"Offers seven straightforward strategies for boys and girls
in the 'tween' years, from understanding what's normal
to handling increased expectations. Very helpful!"
—*The Reader's Edge*

Too OLD FoR THIS,

Too YoUNG FoR THAT!

YoUR SURVIVAL GUIDE FoR
THE MIDDLE-SchooL YEARS

Harriet S. Mosatche, Ph.D., and Karen Unger, M.A.

free spirit
PUBLISHING®

Library of Congress Cataloging-in-Publication Data

Mosatche, Harriet S., 1949–

    Too old for this, too young for that! your survival guide for the middle-school years / Harriet S. Mosatche and Karen Unger ; edited by Elizabeth Verdick

        p. cm.

    Includes bibliographical references and index.

    Summary: Information, advice, and support for middle schoolers on issues such as physical and emotional changes, connecting with friends and family, setting goals, and handling peer pressure.

    ISBN 1-57542-067-8 (pbk.)

    1. Preteens—Life skills guides—Juvenile literature. 2. Preteens—Psychology—Juvenile literature. 3. Middle-school students—Life skills guides—Juvenile literature. 4. Middle-school students—Psychology—Juvenile literature. 5. Teenagers—Life skills guides—Juvenile literature. 6. Adolescent psychology—Juvenile literature. [1. Life skills.] I. Unger, Karen, 1954– II. Verdick, Elizabeth. III. Title.

HQ777.15 .M67 2000
646.7'00835—dc21

                             99-046773

Reading Level Grades 6 & Up; Interest Level Ages 10–14;
Fountas & Pinnell Guided Reading Level Y

20 19 18 17 16 15 14 13 12
Printed in the United States of America
S18860909

Free Spirit Publishing Inc.
217 Fifth Avenue North, Suite 200
Minneapolis, MN 55401-1299
(612) 338-2068
help4kids@freespirit.com
www.freespirit.com

DEDICATION

To my two children who were my kindest listeners and most helpful critics as I wrote this book—Rob, who survived middle school and whose experiences found their way into every chapter, and Liz, who is thriving in middle school and whose wonderful ideas became part of this book.

—H.S.M.

To my son whose biggest challenge in the near future will be to survive preschool but who inspired the idea of a book that both boys and girls would like to read.

—K.U.

ACKNOWLEDGMENTS

We would especially like to acknowledge all of the middle-school kids with whom we spoke and whose quotes appear throughout the book. Thank you so much for your honesty and insights. We also would like to thank Free Spirit Publishing and its founder and publisher Judy Galbraith for offering kids a wealth of books that enlighten families and help kids grow up in not-so-easy times. And we would like to thank our families—our husbands, who supported us as we were immersed in writing and revising, and our parents, who were our guides to surviving not just the teen years, but also the challenges and adventures we have met in our lives.

CONTENTS

LIST of REPRODUCIBLE PAGES

INTRODUCTION

"During my first day of middle school, I couldn't even find the boys' bathroom!
After school, I took the wrong bus and got off at the wrong stop, a mile
from home. My backpack was filled with tons of textbooks, and by the time
I got to my house, my back was aching! But within a week or two,
I'd finally started to adjust."

TIM, 14

Have you noticed that your life seems to be getting more complicated? Do you feel confused and worried one moment, then thrilled and excited the next—as if you're on an ENORMOUS roller coaster, and you don't know how you got there or how to get off, and there's no turning back now?

Welcome to the middle-school years! Like a roller-coaster ride, this time in your life has ups, downs, twists, turns, and sudden starts and stops. Sometimes you may wonder how you can possibly hang on . . . but at least you're not on the ride alone.

Why is middle school so different from elementary school? Because practically everything has changed. Not only do you have more teachers, subjects, homework, projects, and tests, but you might also have a homeroom, a locker, more clubs and activities, and other new things to handle. Your friends and classmates probably don't look, act, or dress the way they used to. Does everyone seem to be talking about the latest couple? Or who's the cutest or coolest, or most popular or athletic?

Life at home may be changing, too. Are your parents suddenly making more rules, giving you more chores, or embarrassing you in front of your friends? Do they sometimes treat you like a child? Do they sometimes expect you to act more grown-up than you feel? You're not a child anymore, but you're not grown-up either. You're in between, and sometimes that's a hard place to be.

If you're between the ages of ten and fourteen, changes are happening to you inside and out. You probably don't think, feel, look, or act like you used to. During these years, you might:

- grow about two to five inches, and gain around five to fifteen pounds per year (which is completely normal but can feel totally weird)
- mature more quickly or slowly than other kids (which is normal, too)
- notice pimples erupting on your face, hair where there was no hair before, and other embarrassing things
- feel excited yet scared about puberty and all the changes that come with it
- worry a lot about making friends, having enough friends, being popular, or finding a boyfriend or girlfriend
- be lost, bored, confused, or frustrated in school
- feel sure that no one on earth totally understands you

With so much happening all at once, who *wouldn't* feel a little overwhelmed?

The middle-school years are unpredictable, but they're also exciting and filled with possibility. You can use this time to:

- explore your talents
- strengthen your skills at school and in athletics and other activities
- learn to understand and deal with your emotions
- build lasting friendships
- form better relationships with the people in your family
- set goals and find ways to reach them
- make plans for your future

The middle-school years are a time when you're figuring out who you are and who you want to be. (This is a lifelong process, by the way, so don't worry if you don't figure it *all* out.) You'll become more of an individual, with your own point of view, and you'll start to find new ways to express yourself—through your activities, schoolwork, clothes, and hobbies. You'll finally be old enough to decide how to spend some of your own money, go more places with your friends (without your parents), and choose which activities to pursue. You get to *do* more and *be* more, and this is the fun part of the middle-school years.

This is a really terrific time in your life. We hope you'll use this book as a guide to make it even better!

ABOUT THIS BOOK

Maybe you're wondering what two adults like us could possibly know about middle school. The answer: plenty. We survived it, just like you will, and we remember what it was like. We know how it feels to be too shy to raise your hand in class, even though you definitely know the answer. Or to be embarrassed beyond belief if your parents pick you up at school and don't wait in the car like you asked them to, or worse yet, if they hug you in front of your friends. Or to get glasses or braces just when you least want them. Or to have a crush on someone who doesn't even know you're alive.

In our careers, we have always been involved in work that concerns kids. Over the years, young people like you have shared with us their experiences, feelings, problems, mistakes, successes, and dreams. We decided to write a book for kids like you, including our own children. Our goal was to create a survival guide for every middle schooler who has ever had questions about all of the new choices and challenges ahead.

If you have any questions or comments about this book, you can write to us in care of:

Free Spirit Publishing Inc.
217 Fifth Avenue North, Suite 200
Minneapolis, MN 55401-1299

Or email us at:
help4kids@freespirit.com

A thirteen-year-old we know once said that life as a middle schooler is fun because you have "more freedom, privileges, and responsibilities," and as an added bonus "you get adult menus at restaurants." We couldn't agree more that life during these years can be fun. There's a lot to look forward to, so enjoy the ride!

GET USED TO YOUR CHANGING BODY

During the middle-school years, one of the biggest changes you and almost all your friends will experience is puberty. Your parents may talk to you about it. You'll probably learn about it in school, read about it, and even watch some videos on the topic. You'll see the kids in your class growing and changing, and you'll experience many of the same changes yourself. Still, puberty can be confusing, and you may have lots of questions you're too embarrassed to ask.

What *is* puberty anyway? And why do people go through it?

Puberty is a time when your body begins the passage into adulthood.

Before you start seeing physical changes on the outside, your body starts to change on the inside. Your brain and certain glands begin to release larger amounts of hormones (powerful chemical substances) into your bloodstream. These hormones play an important role in your body's development.

There's no way to predict *exactly* when you'll start going through puberty (nobody's born with a personal calendar marked with the specific date that puberty begins or ends). Puberty isn't a single event or something that happens overnight. It's a process that lasts for several years, which is why it's a good idea to get used to your changing body.

YOU'RE CHANGING INSIDE AND OUT

When you start puberty, your body begins to grow faster than at any other time—with the exception of your first year of life. Back then, your brain and body were developing rapidly, and the same is true now. Your appetite might increase, as well as your need for sleep. That's because your growing body requires lots of both rest and nutrients to support all the physical changes it's going through.

> "If you're going through puberty at a different rate than your friends are, you might feel uncomfortable because you don't know who to talk to about what's happening. And sometimes, you might feel too small or too big or too gangly. But there's a good part—your parents start to see you as more grown-up, and they let you do more stuff."
>
> **ZOE, 12**

Once you start puberty, you may notice that your shirtsleeves are getting shorter, or your socks are now sticking out below your pants. Is your entire wardrobe shrinking? No, what you're experiencing is known as a growth spurt. Your feet may seem to grow by as much as a shoe size each month, or your hands may grasp a basketball with greater ease. The middle-school years are filled with these kinds of surprises.

Keep in mind that you may start changing earlier or later, and more quickly or slowly than other kids. You'll develop at your own rate—you're growing at a pace that's right for *you*.

Changes in Boys

Boys start going through puberty anywhere from about ages ten to fifteen, and the first sign is usually a major growth spurt. You'll be growing in inches and pounds, and you may start to hear, "You're getting so tall!" or "Look how big you are!" from relatives or other people who haven't seen you for a while.

You'll also notice your voice beginning to deepen. Many boys welcome this change because they sound more masculine for the first time (and they've gotten tired of being confused with their sisters when they answer the phone). Voice changes—like all the other changes of puberty—don't occur all at once. Changes in the voice take place gradually and may involve a lot of squeaking and croaking. You may be embarrassed if your voice cracks when you're answering a question out loud in class. These embarrassing moments can happen to *any* guy your age.

Other changes for boys during puberty include:

- the appearance of underarm and facial hair
- an increase in body hair
- the lengthening and widening of the penis
- the enlargement of the testes
- the growth of pubic hair (it gradually becomes darker and curlier)

- more frequent erections (meaning the penis fills with blood and becomes hard)
- the first ejaculation (release of semen, the fluid containing sperm)
- nocturnal emissions, also known as "wet dreams," meaning ejaculation during sleep

All of these changes are normal, and they take place *gradually*. They also occur at a different pace for every boy.

You may still have questions about the changes you're going through or even doubt whether you're developing in a "normal" way. Talk to an adult you trust—a parent, close relative, teacher, or coach, for example.

From Boys to Men: All About Adolescence and You by Michael Gurian (New York: Price Stern Sloan, 1999). The author offers lots of information, advice, and support in this helpful book. He also answers questions about many things you might be too embarrassed to talk with someone about.

What's Going on Down There? Answers to Questions Boys Find Hard to Ask by Karen Gravelle (New York: Walker & Co., 1998). This lively book covers all the changes that boys experience during puberty. You'll find sections on physical development, feelings, sexual activity, birth control, sexually transmitted diseases (STDs), and much more. It also includes a chapter on girls' changing bodies.

The What's Happening to My Body? Book for Boys by Lynda Madaras (New York: Newmarket Press, 2000). This updated classic has tons of information on boys' bodies and emotions, sexuality, puberty, zits, facial hair, body odor, and more.

Changes in Girls

Generally, girls mature anywhere from ages eight to fifteen—often a couple of years before boys. One of the first signs of puberty is the budding of a girl's breasts, which starts with just a little swelling under the nipples. Breasts come in a wide variety of sizes and shapes, just like penises do. Sometimes one breast may develop more quickly than the other—it's nothing to worry about. Breasts usually even out, but it's unlikely for them to ever look exactly alike. One of yours may always be a bit bigger than the other.

"They have these thin walls in the gym, so we can hear what the boys are saying. They like to talk about the length of their penis. But some girls compare their chest size."

AMELIA, 12

You may start wearing a bra for the first time during the middle-school years. Bra shopping can make any girl nervous at first. Talk about it with your mom or another woman you trust. A knowledgeable salesperson can also help you choose a bra that's the right size for you.

Soon after your breasts begin to develop, you'll start to grow taller and at a faster rate. Your body will become more curvy, and you'll gain weight in your hips, buttocks, and thighs. Don't assume you're getting "fat"—you're not! Your body is taking on a new shape, and an increase in weight at this age is perfectly normal.

Other changes for girls during puberty include:

- the appearance of underarm hair
- the darkening and increasing of arm and leg hair
- the growth of pubic hair (it gradually becomes darker and curlier)
- an increase in discharge from the vagina

One of the biggest changes you'll undergo is menarche, which is the onset of menstruation, or getting your first period. Usually, menarche occurs about one and a half to two years after your breasts begin to grow.

During the menstrual cycle, one of your ovaries (you have two of them) releases an ovum, or egg. It travels through one of your fallopian tubes (you've got two of those as well) to reach the uterus. While the egg travels, the lining of the uterus thickens and fills with extra blood and tissue to prepare for possible fertilization by a sperm. If the egg isn't fertilized, the blood-filled tissue comes apart and passes out of your body through your vagina.

Many girls are afraid that the blood will gush out, maybe during school, and everyone will see it. More likely, your first period will be light, and the blood will look like a brownish stain or just a few drops of red blood. In the beginning, your periods may not occur once a month. It's normal to be irregular for a while. Once your periods become more regular, you can expect them to happen monthly and last anywhere from three to seven days. The first days are the heaviest; the blood flow decreases gradually. You can use tampons or sanitary pads to absorb the blood.

When you have your period, you can do anything you'd normally do: go to school, play sports, swim, shower, take a bath, or whatever. Don't let your period hold you back. You may feel tired or irritable before or during your period, and this is natural. You may also experience cramps, which are actually muscle contractions of the uterus. What can you do about the discomfort? Exercise often helps, and so does getting a bit more rest. If your cramps are severe, talk to a parent, doctor, or school nurse. You may need to take medication to relieve the pain.

Getting your period for the first time may make you feel a mix of emotions: scared, happy, confused, proud, grown-up, worried, or even a little bit sad, because it signals you're leaving childhood behind. You'll probably have a lot of questions about taking care of yourself during your period and handling your feelings. Find someone to talk to—your mom, an aunt, an older sister, a teacher, a coach, or a friend of the family. For more information, take a look at a book or Web site about puberty and getting your period.

It's a Girl Thing: How to Stay Healthy, Safe, and in Charge by Mavis Jukes (New York: Knopf, 1996). This positive and humorous guide to adolescence includes great tips on coping with your changing body, buying your first bra, handling menstruation, and more.

The Period Book: Everything You Don't Want to Ask (But Need to Know) by Karen Gravelle and Jennifer Gravelle (New York: Walker & Co., 1996). Writer Karen Gravelle and her teenage niece, Jennifer, offer lots of straightforward information and advice in this fun book. If you have questions about menstruation, this book can answer them. You'll also find tips on discussing this sensitive topic with parents.

The What's Happening to My Body? Book for Girls by Lynda Madaras (New York: Newmarket Press, 2000). This updated classic covers everything you need to know about puberty and body changes. You'll find helpful information on physical development, menstruation, emotions, sexuality, and much more.

COPING WITH CHANGES

Whether you're a boy or a girl, and no matter where you live, you've got something in common with everyone else your age: body changes. When you look at the other kids in your grade, you'll see that some of the girls tower over the boys, while other girls are smaller. Some girls may have their period or may be wearing a bra, while others haven't developed breasts yet. Some guys may be growing a mustache, while others don't have a hint of facial hair. Some may already have a deep voice, while others haven't experienced voice changes yet. No matter who you are or what stage you're at, change can feel strange.

"I'm glad I finally started growing. I used to be the shortest boy in class."

DAN, 13

It may help to write about the changes and how you feel about them. You can use a journal or notebook, or do this type of writing on a computer. Your words can express *anything*—how you're growing, your emotions, what happened at school on a particular day, your likes and dislikes, your dreams, your goals, and so on. You can also keep track of your body changes by copying the information below and filling it in.

DATE:

WHAT CHANGED:

WHAT I LIKE ABOUT THE CHANGE:

WHAT I DON'T LIKE ABOUT IT:

HOW I FEEL ABOUT MYSELF TODAY:

JUST FOR FUN

Laughing about body changes is one way to keep from getting too serious about puberty. Try the following activity with a friend.

DIRECTIONS: Photocopy the activity below. Ask a friend to think of a word for each description in the parentheses (without letting your friend see the page). After filling in all the blanks, read the whole thing aloud. Have fun!

This morning, I stood naked in front of a full-length mirror. I noticed my _____ and how
                                        (body part)
_____ it was. I was _____ at
(an adjective)   (an emotion)
what I saw. Then I realized that my _____
                                    (another body part)
had changed. I felt so _____. I imagined
                        (another emotion)
how _____ I would look when I turned
    (an adjective)
_____, I decided that I'd better stop
(a number from 15 to 85)
standing there with no clothes on before
_____ saw me!
(a person)

CHECK IT OUT!

Puberty 101
www.puberty101.com
This site contains helpful information and advice on a range of topics including body changes, sexuality, feeling "normal," and more.

Teenwire
www.teenwire.com
Sponsored by Planned Parenthood, this straightforward site provides clear, helpful information about the physical and emotional changes young people experience during puberty.

TAKING CARE OF YOUR BODY

During the middle-school years, you're starting to make more decisions about food. Maybe you fix your own breakfast, eat a school lunch, make yourself a snack when you get home, and even prepare dinner some nights. You've probably got a little more spending money, too, so you might buy food at the mall or other places where you hang out. Did you know that old saying "You are what you eat" is actually true? If you *eat* healthier, you'll *be* healthier. You have the power to choose to eat right and treat your body well.

> "What I like about middle school is that the food is edible for the first time. The hot dogs don't bounce, and the fries are really good."
>
> **NINA, 11**

You're growing so rapidly that you're probably not surprised to find out you need some extra nutrients during the middle-school years. Greater amounts of protein, for example, are required at your age compared to what you needed as a child. Proteins help supply energy and keep your body tissues healthy. You can get the extra protein you need from meat, poultry, fish, milk, and nuts.

Did you know that calcium is also important during these years? To support your growing bone structure, you'll need even more of this mineral now than you will when you're an adult! It's important to consume lots of milk and other dairy products to get added calcium each day. You'll also find this mineral in broccoli, almonds, and calcium-fortified orange juice.

Another mineral you need is iron. Girls require 50 percent more iron from the time they start puberty until well into adulthood. This is because iron is lost in the menstrual blood flow. Boys need extra iron, too, because during the middle-school years, their blood volume and tissue growth increases. What are some good sources of iron? Red meat, peanut butter, apricots, and dark, leafy green vegetables.

As you start puberty, you'll also need extra amounts of another important nutrient called zinc. Zinc and proteins work together to help you grow taller and stronger. You can get added zinc from chicken, lean meats, dairy products, and whole grains.

Don't be surprised if, these days, you're often hungry or feel wiped out when you haven't eaten. This is your body's way of telling you to give it the nutrients it depends on for proper growth. Because of all the changes your body is undergoing, it's a good idea to eat a variety of healthy foods each day including lots of fruits, vegetables, and whole grains.

The Food Guide Pyramid can help you figure out how to eat right and take care of your growing body. Developed by the U.S. Department of Agriculture, the pyramid identifies the five major food groups: (1) Bread, cereal, rice, and pasta (2) Vegetables (3) Fruits (4) Milk, yogurt, and cheese (5) Meat, poultry, fish, dry beans, eggs, and nuts. There's a sixth group, too: Fats, oils, and sweets. It doesn't count as a major food group because fats have little nutritional value. But fats support the work of other nutrients in your body, and you need to have some fat in your diet to maintain good health. Just remember to keep your fat intake low because you only need a little bit to stay healthy.

THE FOOD PYRAMID

Fats, oils, and sweets group
Eat sparingly

Milk, yogurt, and cheese group
2–3 servings
per day

Meat, poultry, fish, dry beans, eggs, and nuts group
2–3 servings
per day

Vegetable group
3–5 servings
per day

Fruit group
2–4 servings
per day

Bread, cereal, rice, and pasta group
6–11 servings per day

Adapted from the Food Guide Pyramid of the USDA.

You can photocopy the pyramid and put it on your refrigerator, so you and other people in your family remember to choose healthy foods as often as possible. The pyramid suggests a range of servings for each major food group (see the serving size information below). The amount per day that's right for you depends on many factors, including how old you are, whether you're a preteen or teen boy or girl, and what your activity level is. Most people should eat *at least* the minimum number of servings from the five major food groups. The more active you are, the more servings you'll need. If you want more help figuring out what to eat, talk to your doctor or school nurse.

You can use the following guidelines to determine what a serving size means for common foods:

BREAD, CEREAL, RICE, AND PASTA GROUP (6–11 servings)
1 slice of bread
1/2 bagel or English muffin
1 oz. of cold cereal
1/2 cup cooked pasta
1/2 cup cooked rice

VEGETABLE GROUP (3–5 servings)
1 cup raw leafy greens such as spinach or lettuce
1/2 cup cooked vegetables or chopped raw vegetables

FRUIT GROUP (2–4 servings)
1 medium orange, apple, or banana
1/2 cup diced, canned, or cooked fruit
3/4 cup of 100% fruit juice
1/2 cup small fruit such as berries or grapes

MILK, YOGURT, AND CHEESE GROUP (2–3 servings)
1 cup milk
1 cup yogurt
1 1/2 oz. of natural cheese
2 oz. of processed cheese

MEAT, POULTRY, FISH, DRY BEANS, EGGS, AND NUTS GROUP (2–3 servings)
2–3 oz. of cooked lean meat such as poultry or fish
1 egg
2 tablespoons of peanut butter
1/3 cup of nuts

FATS, OILS, AND SWEETS GROUP (Eat sparingly)

You don't have to measure every bit of food you put in your mouth. The pyramid is simply a way to make the path to good nutrition less complicated. If you follow it, you shouldn't have a problem getting the nutrients you need.

CHECK IT OUT!

The U.S. Department of Agriculture Web Site for Kids
www.mypyramid.gov/kids
Packed full of activities, this site contains helpful information about food, nutrition, and the food pyramid.

Dieting Dangers

During puberty, you may become more concerned about your weight. You're growing and changing every day, and gaining weight is a normal part of the process. One of the best things you can do for yourself is to avoid obsessing about your weight and body size. Instead, try to accept and appreciate your body and all the changes it's going through.

How do you know if you're at a healthy weight? Ask yourself if you eat sensibly, have lots of natural energy, and feel healthy and balanced. Often, this is a better measure of your health and weight than a number on the bathroom scale. Avoid comparing your weight or body size to your friends' or other people's. Everybody—every *body*—is different. What's right for someone else isn't necessarily right for *you*. If you have concerns about your weight, talk to your doctor or school nurse to get more information.

Starting in the middle-school years, some kids develop problems with eating. You may have heard or read something about eating disorders, which affect both girls and boys (although more girls than boys have problems with them). There are three main types of eating disorders: *anorexia nervosa, bulimia nervosa,* and *compulsive overeating.*

A person with anorexia starves to stay thin and may also exercise excessively to burn off calories. Because of a distorted body image, someone with anorexia looks in the mirror and imagines fat where there isn't any. Without treatment, the person may develop severe health problems, or even die from starvation.

The main symptom of bulimia is bingeing and purging, which means eating a great deal of food, and then vomiting or taking laxatives afterward. Bulimia, like anorexia, may also involve exercising to excess. While a person with anorexia may eat very little, a person with bulimia may appear to eat normally, knowing the food will be purged. As with anorexia, severe health problems may result.

Compulsive overeating, like bulimia, includes bingeing. Someone who's a compulsive overeater may eat average-sized portions in front of other people, but then binge while alone. Overeating like this can lead to serious weight gain. Often, someone who compulsively overeats uses food to soothe painful feelings.

One result of compulsive overeating is obesity, which means being extremely overweight. During the middle-school years, kids who are overweight may be teased or treated as outcasts, which can lead to feelings of loneliness. Compulsive overeaters then turn to food for comfort, leading to further weight gain. Like anorexia or bulimia, this disorder requires treatment from an expert.

All three of these eating disorders can progress to a point where they're life-threatening. What they have in common is *secrecy.* Someone who has problems with food may avoid sitting in the cafeteria, disappear into the bathroom after every meal, hide food in a closet or some other place, or obsess about maintaining a certain weight for activities like wrestling, gymnastics, or ballet. If you suspect that someone you know has an eating disorder, talk to an adult you trust. If you're having problems with food, get help right away. Telling your mom or dad what's going on can be scary, but reaching out is the first step toward getting help and support.

National Eating Disorders Association
www.nationaleatingdisorders.org
(206) 382-3587
The National Eating Disorders Association strives to eliminate eating disorders and body dissatisfaction through education, prevention, and support. Their Web site offers tips for helping affected individuals deal with eating problems, educational materials for schools and organizations, access to prevention programs, and treatment referrals for doctors, therapists, and support groups.

Overeaters Anonymous
www.oa.org
(505) 891-2664
Overeaters Anonymous is a twelve-step program for people recovering from compulsive overeating. Meetings and other tools provide members with a community of support, strength, and hope. Overeaters Anonymous addresses the physical, emotional, and spiritual aspects of the disorder.

Something Fishy
www.something-fishy.org
This site is for people who suffer from anorexia, bulimia, compulsive overeating, and binge eating disorders. It offers information and support, and answers the tough questions you and others may have about eating disorders.

Move That Body

Can you solve this "problem"?

eating right + **X** = a healthy body
X = ?

The answer? *E**X**ercise!*

Exercise is good for your heart, lungs, muscles, bones, and other vital body parts—even your skin and hair. Physical movement makes you think, look, and feel better, too. There's no downside to staying active.

Exercise isn't about sculpting your body into the "perfect" shape. Think of exercise as an important part of taking good care of yourself. When you work out, focus on having fun and challenging your body.

Experts have found that too many preteens and teens today are "couch potatoes." According to the U.S. Surgeon General, young people are spending too much of their free time watching TV, using the computer, and playing video games. And this means less time running around outdoors or playing sports. The result? Decreased physical fitness.

Want to know what being fit really means?

> You can tackle the day's challenges and have plenty of energy left for play.

> Your heart, lungs, bones, and muscles are strong.

> Your body is firm and flexible.

> Your percentage of body fat is low, and your weight is within a normal range.

> You feel good about yourself and have a positive outlook on life.

If you want to be healthy and fit, and give your body the best chance to grow properly, make exercise a regular part of your routine. Get involved in a sport (see pages 146–150 for more information) or find another type of physical activity you enjoy, such as inline skating, dance, karate, biking, or skateboarding. Spend time outdoors hiking, walking your dog, or playing catch. You can still enjoy television, video games, and the computer—just make an effort to avoid sitting for hours at a time, and get up every so often to stretch or do something physical.

Added bonus: All this exercise is good for your brain, too. Studies have shown that kids who are active perform better on tests!

Sweating It out

While we're on the topic of exercise, this might be a good time to talk about sweat. When you reach puberty, your sweat glands become more active. Maybe you used to be able to play an hour of basketball and come off the court smelling like a rose—or at least like a person—but now your jump shot isn't all everyone's noticing. Body odor is one of the changes that may signal to you—and others—that you're going through puberty. Hormones have a lot to do with this. They affect the glands under your arms, which release some not-so-sweet-smelling chemicals when you sweat.

The best way to smell clean is to stay clean. Take a shower or bath every day, and wash up again after exercising. You can also use a deodorant or an antiperspirant. Both help mask odors, but an antiperspirant also helps to decrease the amount you sweat. Many of these products build up their effectiveness, so if you forget to put some on one day because you're late for school, you're still getting a little protection.

As long as you're thinking about odor, consider your feet. After a few hours in sweaty sneakers, the smell of your feet might make even your closest friends keep their distance. Air out your athletic shoes after every use and sprinkle baking soda inside them to keep them fresh. Instead of wearing the same shoes to school every day, give one pair a rest and put on another pair for a couple of days.

To protect your feet from a common fungus known as athlete's foot, keep them clean and dry. If you shower at school after gym, wear flip-flops or other waterproof footwear to prevent catching any fungus that's been left on the floor by someone else. Athlete's foot, which causes very itchy feet, can be treated with over-the-counter medications.

One last thing: An easy, but often forgotten, way to stay healthy and clean is by washing your hands. Get into the habit of washing up before meals, after touching dirty surfaces, and after using the bathroom. Good old soap and water help to stop the spread of germs that cause colds and serious illnesses.

Invasion of the Zits

You may never have thought that much about your skin until now. Suddenly—zap!—zits are invading your face, back, and maybe even your chest. The pimples that tend to appear during puberty are the result of the oil glands in your skin increasing in both size and activity. If your skin is naturally oily, you're likely to experience more breakouts than if your skin is on the dry side. Ask your parents what their skin looked like when they were your age (yes, parents can pass on the tendency toward pimples or clear skin).

You can go to the drugstore and find lots of cleansers, astringents, lotions, and medications designed to clear up pimples or acne. These products can help, and so can keeping your skin clean. Wash your face in the morning, in the evening, and after exercising. Because dirt and oil from your hair can cause pimples on your face, be sure to pull your hair back or wear a cap when you play sports. You may even want to cut your hair shorter or avoid bangs if you tend to get a lot of pimples on your forehead. Avoid picking at pimples because this will only make them worse and may infect them.

There's no absolute way to avoid a breakout, but good skincare can help lessen pimples, whiteheads, and blackheads. Many experts say that eating lots of fresh fruits and vegetables—plus drinking at least six glasses of water each day—leads to clearer skin.

You may notice that on days when you're more stressed out, your skin is oilier and more prone to getting zits. You may feel better knowing that pimples don't last forever, and they're one more sign of growing up. By the end of adolescence, your skin most likely will be clearer. If you have a severe case of acne, ask about making an appointment with a dermatologist (a doctor who specializes in skin problems). A dermatologist can prescribe acne medications.

Protecting your skin with sunscreen is a must when you're outdoors—even if it's cloudy. Use a product with a skin protection factor (SPF) of at least fifteen. Research by the American Cancer Society has shown that to avoid sunburn, you need to reapply sunscreen frequently, particularly if you've been sweating a lot or have been swimming. If you're outdoors during the middle of the day when the sun's at its brightest, wear a hat or baseball cap to shade your face and scalp.

Some people think that exposure to the sun helps clear up zits, plus gives you a "healthy" tan. No way! When your skin darkens or reddens after you've spent time in the sun, this is a sign of damage. Your skin can freckle, darken, or burn when exposed to the sun's ultraviolet (UV) rays whether or not you're fair-skinned, so it's best to protect yourself. Start taking good care of your skin now, and you'll thank yourself in ten, fifteen, or twenty years, when all the signs of sun damage are more likely to show up.

CHECK IT OUT!

The American Academy of Dermatology
www.aad.org
This Web site provides lots of information about skincare. The Acne section (*www.aad.org/public/Publications/pamphlets/Acne.htm*) gives the facts about acne: what causes it, who gets it, and how to treat it. To locate a skin doctor in your area, check out the "Find a Dermatologist" feature.

Catch Some Zzzzzzzzzs

Did you know that about one-third of your life is spent sleeping? Sleep is an essential part of life—without it, human beings can't function.

When you sleep, your mind and body are at rest, and this allows you to preserve the energy you'll need during the day. Most people need about eight hours of sleep each night, but during the preteen and teen years, even more sleep is required. Why? Because during sleep, your pituitary gland (located in your brain) releases large amounts of growth hormones. If you want to grow at the highest rate possible for you, make an effort to get a good night's rest. You may need to take a nap after school sometimes to refresh yourself before a night of homework.

> "During the school week, I have to get up at 7 A.M. I wish school would start later. Sometimes I feel like I'm drifting off in class. I do fall asleep in school once in a while (and I'm not the only one)!"
>
> **KEVIN, 13**

When you get enough sleep, you're more alert in the morning. You'll have more energy and be able to concentrate better. And that means you'll be at your best each day!

One of the questions that kids in middle school often have is, "Am I normal?" Keep in mind that "normal" covers a wide range. You may be a head taller or shorter than every other kid in your class. You may have more or less body hair, zits, or muscles than your friends. You may experience wet dreams or periods long before or after other kids your age. You may show all the signs of puberty described in this chapter or none of them . . . yet. The bottom line is you're developing in your own way and at your own rate—and that's just the way it should be. You're a unique individual. If all of the body changes are making you wonder and ask questions, that's just a normal reaction to growing up!

LIKE THE SKIN
YOU'RE IN

How do you feel when you look in the mirror? Good? Bad? So-so? Happy one day and then not so happy the next? Like most middle schoolers, your feelings about your appearance may change from day to day, or even hour to hour. At this stage of your life, it's natural to be more aware of how you look, and to care more, too.

Survival tip #2 is about learning to like the skin you're in. What does this mean? You're an individual, your own unique person. All your different parts—from head to toe—make up the whole of you. Because you're going through lots of physical changes, you may have doubts about your looks. You may even start to believe your appearance is a measure of who you are as a person. Not so!

You've probably heard this before, but it's worth saying again: *Looks aren't everything.* How you look is a very small piece of the total you. You are also your mind, heart, skills, interests, abilities, thoughts, feelings, accomplishments, dreams, values, talents, personality, experiences, culture, and more. These days, your outside package may seem really important to you. But keep in mind what's *inside* counts more. And self-esteem is where it all begins.

WHAT'S SELF-ESTEEM?

SELF-ESTEEM (noun): confidence and
satisfaction in oneself; pride; self-respect.

Your self-esteem is a measure of how you feel about yourself. When you're proud of who you are, you've got healthy self-esteem.

Here are some things that can make you feel good about yourself:

Caring about other people.

Treating others with kindness and respect.

Caring about yourself.

Treating yourself with kindness and respect.

Being cared about by people who matter to you.

Being treated with kindness and respect
by the people you care about.

The stronger your self-esteem is, the stronger *you* are. And this means:

1. You can face life's challenges with a positive attitude.
2. You set realistic goals for yourself, instead of aiming too high or too low.
3. You're motivated to achieve and take action to reach your goals.

4. You're more likely to take positive risks because you believe you can succeed.

5. You're less likely to take negative risks because you respect yourself and don't want to put yourself in danger.

6. You're more likely to resist negative peer pressure, which means you won't go along with the crowd just to fit in.

7. You can bounce back when you make mistakes or face disappointments.

8. You can recognize and appreciate someone else's strengths and accomplishments.

9. You don't need to see someone else fail to feel good about yourself.

10. You can let yourself be happy because you know you're worth it.

Believing in yourself is a big challenge during the middle-school years. Research shows that between the ages of ten and fourteen, lots of kids (especially girls) experience SHRINKING self-esteem. This "vanishing act" might leave you questioning your decisions, abilities, and smarts.

On top of all the new challenges you face at home and at school, your body goes through lots of changes during puberty. At times, you may feel awkward and anxious about your body. And with so much going on, you may find it harder to feel comfortable in your own skin.

"On days when my favorite clothes are in the laundry and my hair makes me look like a jerk, it's hard to feel good about myself. That's when I almost wish I could go back to bed instead of going to school."

STEVE, 12

The middle-school years are a time when looks seem really important. All the kids may be talking about who's cute, or cool, or well-dressed—and who's not. You may start to believe that being attractive is the truest measure of someone's worth. But it isn't!

During puberty, your image of yourself may go up and down each day. In fact, your self-image (how you see yourself) is kind of like a barometer—an instrument that measures the pressure of the atmosphere to predict the weather. A rise in barometric pressure predicts sunny days, while a drop in pressure indicates rain. In a similar way, you might look in the mirror and like what you see one day. But suppose the very next day you get a disastrous haircut? Suddenly your image of yourself goes from sunny to cloudy.

At this point in your development, you still have more growing to do. Your face, body, height, weight—almost everything about your appearance—will change within the next few years. You'll probably even go through what nearly everyone else in the whole world has gone through during puberty: an awkward stage. They survived it, and so will you. It may help to remember a few of the things that *really* make someone attractive:

- a ready smile
- a kind heart
- a good sense of humor

These qualities have nothing to do with appearance.

If you're feeling down about your looks, consider a few things you like about your appearance. Whatever they are, write them in a list called "My Good Points." If you can't think of anything to write, get help from a friend or someone in your family. (You may be surprised at all the positive things this person has to say!) Review your list and give yourself the credit you deserve. And instead of focusing on your so-called flaws, keep reminding yourself of your good points. With time and effort, you'll become more comfortable with your looks. And when you are, other people will feel more comfortable around you.

If you're doubtful about your appearance and these doubts affect other aspects of your life (like school and friendships), ask yourself if you've sprung a self-esteem "leak." To keep your self-esteem healthy, you'll have to watch out for The Self-Esteem Sinkers. Don't let them pull you down!

Self-Esteem Sinkers

- **Worrying about what other people think.** It takes a lot of energy to imagine what everyone's thinking of you. The real question is: What do you think of *yourself?*

- **Comparing yourself negatively to other people.** Remember you're unique. You can look and do things your own way. Let yourself be yourself!

- **Expecting to be perfect.** No one is—why try to be? You're human, which means you'll sometimes make mistakes. So learn from them. Forgive yourself. And move on.

- **Playing the "I'll be happy when . . ." game.** Have you ever told yourself, "I'll be happy only if I make the team" or "I'll finally be happy when I earn an A+" or even "I can't be happy unless I get this CD/shirt/ videotape/bike"? This is one game you can't ever win. Happiness is a *choice* that's yours to make. Let yourself be happy!

Here are some fun ideas for giving your self-esteem a lift:

1. **Create a list of things that make you proud.** A list like this reminds you you're a valuable person—not because you're a hero or a star but because you're *you*. Any time you want to boost your self-esteem, read through the list or add more items to it.

   ## WHAT MAKES ME FEEL PROUD:

   - finishing my homework without being reminded
   - being nice to my sister without wanting something in return
   - organizing my desk to help me get my work done
   - practicing soccer to develop my skills, but not feeling like I have to win every game
   - telling my dad I love him without him saying it first

2. **Practice visualization.** Go someplace private, close your eyes, and imagine a quality you'd like to have or you already have but would like to strengthen. For example, maybe you'd like to be more confident, artistic, or brave. Now imagine—or visualize—a scene in which you're showing this quality. Perhaps you'll envision yourself confidently taking a test, painting an amazing picture, or doing a stunt on your skateboard. Visualization means you start with imagination and end up with a better image of yourself. You can use this technique every day, if you'd like.

3. **Set a goal.** What do you really want to accomplish? Is there something you dream of doing someday? If you want to achieve in life, start by setting a goal—something you know you can reach if you really work at it. (You can read more about goal setting on pages 169–172.) Congratulate yourself when you reach your first goal, and then set another . . . and another!

4. **Exercise regularly.** Physical activity does more than get you in shape—it also helps you feel good. That's because exercise releases endorphins (brain chemicals) that give you a happy, relaxed feeling. Experts say people who exercise on a regular basis feel more positive about themselves.

5. **Learn to stand up for yourself.** (This is also known as acting in an assertive way.) You'll feel better about yourself if you know how to express your opinion and let your voice be heard. You don't have to allow other people to take advantage of you, tease you, or push you around. Sticking up for yourself can be a challenge, but the more you do it, the easier it gets! (Read more about this on pages 115–117.)

6. **Find meaningful quotes that make you feel good.** You can look for quotes in books, magazines, or even fortune cookies. Keep the quotes someplace where you'll see them often—on your desk, bulletin board, or mirror, for example. You can also store them in a journal or inside the front cover of a school notebook.

7. **Give yourself little gifts.** Being good to yourself this way reminds you you're worth taking care of. Every so often, buy yourself a small present— something for your hobby or collection, for example. The gift doesn't have to be expensive to make you feel good.

Stick Up for Yourself! Every Kid's Guide to Personal Power and Positive Self-Esteem by Gershen Kaufman, Ph.D., Lev Raphael, Ph.D., and Pamela Espeland (Minneapolis: Free Spirit Publishing Inc., 1999). This revised and updated edition of a classic helps you learn about yourself and what's important to you—plus offers tips on raising your self-esteem and being a more assertive person.

POSITIVE THINKING

Do you have a familiar voice talking to you inside your head? Most people do. Is this voice positive or negative? Is it more likely to say, "I'm ugly" or "Lookin' good!"? You may not realize how much your self-talk (that's what talking to yourself this way is called) influences how you feel and act.

Thinking *positive* thoughts is a way to feel better and stronger inside. But maybe you're used to always hearing a negative voice inside your head. Does your self-talk sound something like this?

Negative thinking and negative self-talk can lower your self-esteem. When your head is filled with negatives, you're less likely to take risks or achieve results you can be proud of. (Because why try anything if you've already predicted you'll fail?) Then, when you do fail, you probably tell yourself, "See, I knew I couldn't do it." This is known as a self-fulfilling prophecy.

You have the power to turn any situation around by thinking about it positively. Why not give positive thinking and self-talk a try? Next time you're facing a situation like the ones described below, make an effort to listen to the voice in your head. If you replace negative words with positive ones, you'll notice a difference in how you feel. And with practice, you'll get better at seeing yourself—and your life—in a brighter light. That's known as the power of positive thinking!

Before a test
Instead of: "I know I'll fail."
Tell yourself: "I'll study hard and do my best."

During class
Instead of: "If I say the wrong answer, they'll think I'm dumb."
Tell yourself: "I'll give it my best shot. If I get the answer wrong, I'll find out why."

If you make a mistake
Instead of: "I can't do anything right."
Tell yourself: "Mistakes are a chance to learn."

When you meet new people
Instead of: "They won't like me."
Tell yourself: "I can help them get to know me better."

Before the school dance
Instead of: "No one will dance with me because I'm not cute enough."
Tell yourself: "If I go with my friends, we'll have fun. Plus, *I* can do the asking!"

When a friend or family member encourages you
to try something new
Instead of: "I'm going to look bad if I can't do it right."
Tell yourself: "It will be fun to learn a new skill."

If someone compliments you
Instead of: "This person must be crazy to say that."
Tell yourself: "How nice of that person to notice."

If your plans get canceled
Instead of: "Now I'll be bored the rest of the day."
Tell yourself: "This gives me a chance to work on my hobby or other activities."

When you look in the mirror
Instead of: "Nothing looks good on me."
Tell yourself: "I'll put on something that makes me feel good."

From now on, every time you hear that negative "inner critic" saying something that sounds like it came from your worst enemy, substitute different words—ones that might come from your most ardent admirer or closest friend. That's positive self-talk in action!

GETTING GLASSES AND BRACING FOR BRACES

Just when you start caring a lot more about your appearance, your dentist may recommend a visit to the orthodontist. Lots of kids (and adults, too) need braces to straighten their teeth.

Braces aren't something to get totally stressed about. They're temporary—you won't have to wear them forever. You may wonder if braces will hurt, or whether other people will think you look weird wearing them, or if the braces will make it impossible for you to kiss anyone with confidence. Here are the facts:

- Braces hurt a little when you first get them on (and every time you get them tightened).
- Your teeth may ache for a few days afterward.
- The wires take some getting used to.

A short list
of famous
"metal mouths":

Actress **Claire Danes** has had braces, and so has teen tennis pro **Venus Williams.**

Cher once wore braces for a photo in *People* magazine.

Brett Favre, quarterback of the 1996 Super Bowl champion Green Bay Packers, wore braces at the height of his NFL career.

Chelsea Clinton wore them for over a year while her dad was president.

Will everyone stare at your newly shiny mouth? There's no way to predict exactly how other people will react, but most likely, they'll notice the change. After a while, people will get used to seeing you in braces, and it won't be a big deal. As for kissing, that's almost always a big deal—whether you wear braces or not! See pages 121–123 for more about puckering up.

Some kids like traditional silver braces, while others prefer clear ones or colorful wires. It's up to you to choose braces that fit your style. You can even change the colors of the wires to match the season or a special holiday.

Depending on what your orthodontist recommends, you may need to wear a headgear that attaches to your braces and hooks around your neck or over your head. Most likely, you can put on your headgear at night before you go to bed. Or you may need to wear small rubber bands that attach to little hooks on your braces. Usually, one rubber band connects the top wire to the bottom wire on each side of your mouth. Just be careful not to open your mouth too wide, which could cause the rubber band to break or to shoot out of your mouth.

The most important thing to know about braces is that when you have them, you've got to take extra care of your teeth. Make sure you brush carefully. You may want to keep a toothbrush and toothpaste at school so you can brush after lunch. Your orthodontist may suggest a toothbrush specially designed to reach around the wires in your mouth. He or she may also tell you to stay away from sticky snacks like dried fruit, bubblegum, and licorice, which can get caught in your braces or bend the wires.

Once your braces are removed, you usually have to wear a retainer for a while. Retainers are made of plastic and sometimes combined with wire, and they're molded to the shape of your teeth. Since you probably need to remove your retainer when you eat or if you play a sport or musical instrument, make sure you don't accidentally throw it away.

The Orthodontic Information Page
www.bracesinfo.com
This fun site includes lots of facts about braces, a long list of famous people who wear braces, a collection of braces links, and much more. Learn about the history of braces, find orthodontic jokes, and view pictures of people with braces.

Around this time, you may also see another type of specialist: an eye doctor (an ophthalmologist or an optometrist). An eye doctor can help you figure out if you need to get glasses, or if you should have your current prescription adjusted. You may decide you're ready for contact lenses, and your parents and doctor can help you determine if and when these lenses are right for you. If you play sports, you may be required to wear special sports glasses or goggles for protection.

Whether you need glasses, contacts, or goggles, follow these two rules: *Wear them* and *take care of them.* Lots of people (all ages) forget how important it is to put on their glasses or contacts, and keep them clean. You may sometimes think it's a pain to wear glasses or soak your contact lenses, but you'll feel better—and *see* better—if you do.

If you've never worn glasses before, you might be self-conscious about getting a pair. As with braces, people may notice the change and comment on it. Eventually, they'll get used to seeing you in glasses. When you go to pick out your frames, bring along a friend or two to get another opinion. It can be fun to choose glasses that express your own style!

HAIRCARE AND OTHER PERSONAL MATTERS

You may notice that your hair is getting oilier, which is normal during puberty. Or that you've got a few "flakes," otherwise known as dandruff. You can use products for oily hair or a dandruff problem. You may also need to shampoo your hair more often—even every day.

If you have a hairstyle that requires constant maintenance (as in you can't pass by a mirror without whipping out your comb, gel, and spray) or if most of the morning is dedicated to your hair, it may be time to make a change. Go for a simpler style, so you don't have to spend a lot of time on it. Likewise, if you're known at school as "bedhead," you may want to put more energy into combing or brushing. Good grooming is one way to show you care about yourself.

CHECK IT OUT!

Unravel the Secrets of Hair
library.thinkquest.org/26829/i_e.htm
Written by kids, this site provides fun and surprising facts about hair, a history of hairstyles, hair games and activities, and tips on good haircare. You can even contribute your own hair experiences or artwork to the site.

Some girls you know may be experimenting with makeup. Using cosmetics is a personal choice, but parents usually have something to say about it. Some girls aren't allowed to use makeup until they reach a certain age. Others don't have any restrictions at all. If you're into using it, that's fine, but be sure you know *why* you are. Is it because you want to—or because your friends do? Is it because you like how you look in it—or you can't stand the way you look without it? Is it because you feel good while wearing it—or you think it's important to look older and more mature? Ask yourself what's really right for *you*.

If you decide to use makeup, get some opinions from family members or friends. Keep in mind that models posing on television or in magazine ads use extra-heavy makeup for the camera; if you copy this style, you may look artificial. Instead, go for a more natural look, using just a little blush, lip color, or mascara. One thing to remember about makeup is that wearing it throughout the night can clog your pores. Always wash your face before going to bed.

ouch! A Few Words About Piercing

The middle-school years are a time when you're changing quickly, and you may feel pressured to look older. Your friends and other people your age may be thinking about piercing their ears—and a whole lot more. Are you considering adding a few holes to your earlobes? Or maybe your belly button, nose, tongue, or some other body part?

Some states have started making rules about how old you have to be to get your body pierced. One thing you should know is that piercing can be risky. If the procedure isn't done right, you could get an infection like hepatitis—or worse. Unskilled "piercers" could also cause nerve damage or scarring. Each type of piercing has its own dangers: ear piercing can tear or split the earlobe; nose studs can become buried in the skin; and tongue piercings can cause teeth fractures, swelling, bleeding, damaged cheek tissue, and lisped or slurred speech. Before you get yourself pierced *anywhere,* talk to your mom or dad about the decision. Make sure you've got permission first and you understand the risks.

What About Shaving?

Whether you're a boy or a girl, puberty is the time to make some decisions about shaving. Some boys start shaving the moment they spot a little hair on their upper lip. Other boys decide not to shave because they think they look older with a mustache—no matter how light it is.

Some girls choose to shave their underarms or legs; others prefer the natural look. Still others remove unwanted hair by waxing or using a depilatory cream, which contains special hair-removal ingredients. And some girls use a bleaching cream to lighten the hair on their upper lip or on their arms. If you want to try any of these products, be sure to read the directions carefully first.

Most people use razors to remove hair. You can choose a regular razor or an electric shaver. If you're going to use a regular razor, get some basic instructions from someone who has more shaving experience than you do or follow the how-to's below.

The key to a good shave is preparation. If you skip over the prep work, you might look and feel like you shaved with a cheese grater!

Step #1: Choose the right razor for you.

There are a huge variety of razors to choose from. Disposables are usually plastic, and you use them a few times and then throw them away. With a cartridge razor, you keep the razor but buy new blade cartridges whenever the blade needs to be replaced. (Better for the environment.)

What's most important is that the razor is sharp and clean. If you're out of razors or blades, don't borrow someone else's used ones—it's possible to spread skin problems or diseases.

Step #2: Prepare your skin.

Warm water or steam from a bath or shower softens hairs, allowing them to be cut more easily. If you're not going to bathe before you shave, soak your skin with warm, soapy water.

When you're ready to shave, wet your skin with warm water and slather on some shaving cream. Why use shaving cream? The lather softens your hair and lubricates your skin, allowing the blade to glide over it smoothly.

Step #3: Use the proper technique.

Use a light, slow stroke while moving the razor along the surface of your skin. Keep your razor clean as you're using it—rinse it often in warm water to remove clumps of hair or shaving cream.

Step #4: Clean up afterward.

After you've finished shaving, rinse the area with cool water and pat it dry. If you want to use some kind of lotion afterward, avoid alcohol-based products, which can sting or irritate freshly shaven skin. If you're going to use your blade again, rinse it thoroughly and shake off any excess water.

If you're bleeding from a small cut (and that's bound to happen, especially the first couple of times), you can apply a styptic pencil. These white, chalky "pencils" are sort of old-fashioned and they sting like crazy when you apply them, but they work. Or you can use a tried-and-true remedy: tear a tiny piece of tissue paper and stick it on the cut; it will stay there by itself. After a few minutes, moisten the paper and gently peel it off. Don't forget, or you'll end up leaving the house with little pieces of tissue sticking to your skin.

Clothing Matters

You probably know that fashions come and go. What's in one day is totally out the next. Do you often try to match your clothing style to that of your friends or the people you see on TV? Instead, buy clothes that fit you, not the latest trend. Decide what you're comfortable in and choose clothes that feel good. If you're unsure about what you like, it may help to get some advice from your friends or family.

CHECK IT OUT!

Fashion: An Online Newshour Web Site for Students
www.pbs.org/newshour/on2/fashion.html
Produced by PBS, this fun, informative site offers young people lots of information on fashion. You can learn about hairstyles, the history of fashion, fashions at school, the latest high-tech fabrics, and more.

Naturally, your clothes may see a lot of wear and tear. This is why it helps to learn to make some simple repairs. Ask your mom or dad to teach you how to sew on a button or fix a split seam. You can also find out how to use the washer, the dryer, and an iron if you don't know how already. Then simply follow the laundering/ironing instructions on the clothing labels. Taking care of your own laundry not only gives your parents a break but also guarantees your clothes will be clean and ready to wear when you need them.

Want to know some cheap ways to put new life into old clothing? Here are a few ideas:

- Use dyes or fabric paints to cover stains or small rips on clothes and sneakers.
- Wear layers (a T-shirt under another shirt, for example), and try different clothing combinations to give your wardrobe more variety.
- Visit a thrift store or consignment shop for good deals on used clothing. Or raid a family member's closet—with permission, of course—to find something different to wear.
- Accessorize: ties, scarves, buttons, belts, hats, socks, pins, and other accessories are an inexpensive way to make a fashion statement.

Some middle-school kids put a lot of energy into their looks, spending extra money on clothes, shoes, caps, cosmetics, cologne, jewelry, and other accessories. It can be fun to try out different styles and fashions. But sometimes you might feel pressured to appear more grown-up than you really are. Do you ever feel that to be accepted you need to look a certain way or have all the right "stuff"? In middle school, there's more pressure to wear certain brands of clothing—to avoid being labeled or teased. Lots of girls and guys are brand-conscious and feel anxious about owning the right clothes and shoes.

It's easy to get caught up in comparing your own clothes, shoes, watch, haircut, and backpack to everyone else's. But all of this is only as big of a deal as you make it. Stuff is just stuff. Having more or less of it doesn't make you more or less of a person.

Did you know that a lot of adults are interested in how you look and what you buy—but they *aren't* your parents, teachers, or anyone else you know? Marketers, ad writers, product developers, magazine editors, and owners of popular clothing stores want to sell you things: clothes, shoes, cosmetics, an image. All of these people have even come up with a name for you: *tween* (not yet a teen, not a child—somewhere in be*tween*).

Teen magazines are filled with fashion advice, beauty tips, and articles on how and how not to dress. These magazines also contain tons of clothing advertisements, all of which are sending you some very strong messages about how to look. Even if you don't read these magazines, you're probably seeing lots of appearance-related ads on TV or online. Some experts believe you may be exposed to 400 to 600 ads every day! These ads come through all forms of media: newspapers, television, Web sites, billboards, videos, video games, computer games, magazines, and movies.

Even when you were younger, you received media messages. You may not think of toys as "media," but in a way they are. Toys like fashion dolls and action figures often carry certain messages and meanings. If you're a girl, you probably played with fashion dolls when you were younger, and if you're a boy maybe you did, too. But did you ever think about the way the dolls look? Their body shape—whether they're tall, skinny, small-waisted, and big-chested female dolls or tall, lean, hugely muscled male dolls—isn't at all realistic for most people.

Action figures pass along the same unrealistic messages about looks as fashion dolls do. In fact, over the years, these toys have gotten more and more muscular. A boy or man with the measurements of some of today's action figures would have a 57-inch chest, a 30-inch waist, and 27-inch biceps—impossible for a human being!

IF YOU WERE A FASHION DOLL ...

IF YOU WERE AN ACTION FIGURE ...

Whether you were aware of it as a child or not, the body-shape messages were there. And they still are today, though in a different form. These days, you probably look up to actors, models, musicians, and sports stars. There's nothing wrong with admiring celebrities—many people do. But the admiration may turn into something more. You might feel like you *have* to look like a celebrity to look good. (Not true!)

Here's the truth behind all the glamour:

- **Celebrities** have "tricks" for making themselves more attractive, such as using fashion consultants, makeup artists, hairstylists, and cosmetic surgeons. In addition, many celebrities diet or exercise way too much in pursuit of thinner bodies.
- **Television actors** and **models** rely on professionally applied makeup, special lighting, and flattering camera angles. If you saw these people in person, the makeup on their faces would look strange.
- **Magazine models** have their photos touched up and improved by computer technology. Computers can subtract pounds and completely change the look of people's hair, eyes, and skin.
- **Professional athletes** spend tremendous amounts of time building their bodies with the help of trainers, team doctors, and other professionals who help monitor the athletes' weight, health, and fitness level.

If you were a fly on the wall at the home of your favorite star, you'd get a glimpse of the person without all the "perfect" hair, makeup, lighting, and clothes. And you know what? He or she would look like a normal person—someone who has some good points and some not-so-good ones, just like the rest of us. Don't let yourself get caught up in all the hype.

Just for fun, try the following activity with a friend. Ask your parents if you can see yearbooks from their high-school days. You may be surprised by who was considered attractive. You can also go to your local library and look at old issues of fashion and beauty magazines (anywhere from 10 to 100 years back, depending on your library's resources). What do you think of the clothes, hair, makeup, and shoes? How about the fashion and beauty advice?

Keep in mind that, in the future, any kid glancing at today's portrayal of "the fifty best-looking people" may wonder why everyone had such bizarre taste!

If you've ever expressed doubts about your appearance, maybe your parents or other adults in your life responded with, "Looks don't matter." And if looks don't matter, you might have wondered why so many adults seem preoccupied with their appearance. To confuse matters, you see attractive kids, teens, and grown-ups on TV and in movies, magazines, and catalogs, and maybe you want to look like these people. The message you're receiving from them is, "Looks *do* matter."

So, what are you supposed to believe? The answer: believe in *yourself.*

Sure, looks matter somewhat—otherwise why would people bother to wash, shave, fix their hair, put on attractive clothes, or do anything to improve their appearance? Taking good care of your body, skin, hair, and teeth are all positive steps toward looking and feeling your best. But another important step is taking care of your self-esteem.

UNDERSTAND

YOUR FEELINGS

Stormy. *Changing. Extreme.* Are we talking about the weather? Nope, we're talking about moods.

These days, you may be dealing with lots of emotional highs and lows. One moment you might feel great, and the next you're bummed out. Mood swings are common during the middle-school years.

Sometimes your mom or dad might say you're moody or blame your hormones for your emotional ups and downs. Hormones play a part in how you feel, but research shows they're not the only cause of mood swings. Because the middle-school years mean added responsibilities at home, at school, and with friends, you might sometimes feel stretched to your limit. And you probably expect more from yourself these days, too. You're older now, and you're facing new challenges and decisions. The pressures can be tough to handle, making you feel frustrated sometimes. But the opposite happens, too—when you successfully handle a new challenge, you're probably excited and proud of your achievement.

Once in a while, the intensity of your emotions might surprise or even scare you. Survival tip #3 can help you understand and cope with your moods and feelings. When you know what you're feeling and why, you're better prepared to handle your emotions in healthy ways.

WHAT ARE YOU FEELING?

Here's an activity that can help you figure out the feelings certain events might bring about. You'll need paper and something to write with.

DIRECTIONS: Read through each situation and think about whether you've had a similar experience. Write about how you felt at the time. If you haven't been in some of the following situations, try to imagine how you'd feel if you had been, and write about that.

- The big game is about to begin. Your team has won the last ten games, and another victory means you'll set a league record.
- Your teacher says, "I'm going to have to call your parents if you continue to do poorly on your tests."

- The person you have a crush on asks you to go to the school dance.
- You hear your dad tell your sister how proud he is of her grades.
- The auditions for the school talent show are being held tomorrow, and you've rehearsed your routine as much as possible.
- Your mom tells you to go to bed, but your favorite TV show won't be over for another twenty minutes.
- You wake up on a Friday morning and find out school's canceled due to a snowstorm.
- Everyone's changing for gym, including you.
- For the first time, you've completed every answer in a really difficult crossword puzzle.
- The referee makes a bad call against you.
- A new friend unexpectedly says, "You're so cool!"

Writing about your emotions helps you express them. You can write about your moods and feelings in a journal or notebook; another option is to work on a computer. Use the following idea starters if you need help thinking of what to write:

DATE:

WHAT I'M FEELING:

WHY I FEEL THIS WAY:

HOW I EXPRESSED THIS EMOTION:

WAYS TO HELP MYSELF FEEL
BETTER WHEN I'M DOWN:

At first, it might feel weird to write about your feelings, especially if you're worried that someone might read what you wrote. You don't have to show your words to *anyone,* even your best friend, unless you want to. Keep your journal or notebook in a place that only YOU know about, like in the back of your closet or even in a trunk or safe that has a lock on it. If you write on the computer, store your files on disks and keep them in a private place. This way, you won't have to worry about anyone sneaking a peek.

Another good way to release your feelings is by talking about them. You can have a conversation with a friend or someone else you're close to. Sometimes, it's best to go to an adult, especially if you're feeling really confused, hurt, or alone. You might talk to a parent, a teacher, your principal, a school counselor, an advisor, a school nurse, a youth group leader, your coach, or a religious leader. These adults can help you figure out what you're feeling and why—and offer you the support you need.

When you're feeling very strong emotions, it's hard to think clearly about the adults who might help you out. So the time to identify specific people who can offer support is *before* you're in a crisis. How about right now? Take a moment to ask yourself these questions:

- Who do I feel comfortable sharing my feelings with?
- Who has given me support in the past?
- Who's good at giving helpful advice?
- Who do I trust with my innermost thoughts?
- Who really listens to what I have to say?
- Who is sensitive and kind?

Can you think of at least a couple of adults you trust and feel comfortable sharing your feelings with? It's a good idea to identify several people, in case one of them isn't available. That way, you've got a backup person when you need one.

Now the question is, how do you start an important conversation with one of them? Here are some suggestions:

- "This is hard for me to talk about but . . ."
- "I need to talk about some things I'm feeling right now. Do you have time to listen?"
- "I'm feeling uncomfortable about sharing this . . ."
- "Sometimes I feel so (angry, sad, upset, worried) that I don't know what to do. Can you give me some advice?"
- "Is this a good time for us to talk about something important?"
- "I need to share something that's bothering me."

You can adapt the conversation openers above to suit your own personal style. The important thing is to start that conversation. It may seem difficult to talk about your feelings, but most likely, the adult you've chosen to open up to will try to make it easier for you. You picked that individual because of his or her sensitivity, kindness, and willingness to listen. Once you've started to talk, the hardest part of the conversation will be behind you.

CHECK IT OUT!

The Teenage Guy's Survival Guide: The Real Deal on Girls, Growing Up, and Other Guy Stuff by Jeremy Daldry (Boston: Little, Brown and Company, 1999). Guys have emotions, too. As the author of this book says: "They might not like to think they do—but they do. They feel happy, sad, lonely, angry, bitter, and jealous in the same way that everyone else does." If you're a boy and you want some advice on figuring out your emotions and all the other changes you're going through, take a look at this fun, helpful book by a guy who's been there.

Your Emotions, Yourself: A Guide to Your Changing Emotions by Doreen Virtue, Ph.D. (Los Angeles: Lowell House Juvenile, 1996). This reassuring guide for girls explains mood swings, stress, and emotions. You'll learn how to understand your feelings, express them, and feel good about yourself, too.

Dealing with Feelings
www.KidsHealth.org/kid/feeling/index.html
The KidsHealth "Dealing with Feelings" site is mainly devoted to physical health, but it includes lots of information about feelings, too. You'll find articles and advice about your changing body and mind, plus a place to read answers to kids' frequently asked questions.

HOW EMBARRASSING!

Isn't it interesting that hearing about other people's embarrassing moments is hysterically funny, but living through those moments yourself is decidedly *unfunny*?

Embarrassment is the feeling that you've done something really stupid in front of other people. For example, it's embarrassing to

"When I went to a music festival with my friends, one of them decided to pour water on my pants, just for fun. Then when we stood up, he decided it would be a good idea to yell 'Mike, that's what a Porta Potty is for!' At least fifty people turned around to look at me!"

MIKE, 13

find out you've been talking to someone you have a crush on—with a piece of bright green lettuce stuck to your front tooth! Or to realize, in the middle of telling a joke about your science teacher, that she's STANDING RIGHT BEHIND YOU. Want to know one of the best ways to survive an embarrassing moment? Just say, "Whoa, am I embarrassed!" and laugh about it. This works better than pretending nothing happened or hiding your feelings. Laughing at your own mistakes makes them seem smaller.

"I love to dance, but most of the time I'm too shy to dance in front of my friends. One day, I put on a CD that I'd just gotten and started practicing some hip-hop jazz moves. I was really getting into it when, out of the corner of my eye, I caught a glimpse of my brother's friend who had just come into the house looking for him. To make matters worse, all I was wearing was a swimsuit!"

ALI, 12

Kids, parents, teachers, bosses—*everyone* makes mistakes and has embarrassing moments. Even celebrities, presidents, and Olympic-winning athletes. It's not the end of the world, even though it may seem like that at the time.

Think about how you usually react when someone else has an embarrassing moment. Do you double over with laughter? Do you tease the person about it? When you see someone else make a mistake, do what you can to smooth it over. That's what you'd want somebody else to do for you.

COPING WITH STRESS

Rrrriiiiinnnng!!!! The alarm clock startles you awake. You can't find your favorite T-shirt, your brother gets to the bathroom first and locks the door (and he's not going to rush on your account), your mom's running around because she's late for work, and you accidentally spill the milk all over the table instead of pouring it on your cereal. It's not even eight in the morning, and already you're feeling completely stressed out. Sound familiar?

Have the adults in your life ever said anything like this to you?

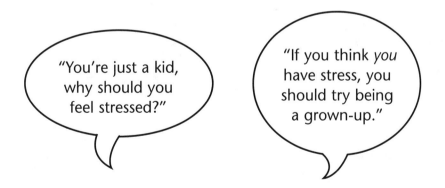

"You're just a kid, why should you feel stressed?"

"If you think *you* have stress, you should try being a grown-up."

    The fact is, being a kid doesn't prevent you from experiencing stress. Many middle-school kids feel anxious about body changes, friendships, grades, tests, and family issues. Do these things cause stress in your life? Ask your mom, your dad, or your friends what leaves them feeling stressed. Maybe some of their answers will surprise you. Or maybe you'll find out that you worry about many of the same things. Either way, it can be reassuring to know you're not the only one feeling anxious.

Stress causes natural physical reactions in your body. That's because when you're under pressure or in danger, your body is programmed to fight or run away. Experts call this the "fight-or-flight response." While not every person has the exact same reactions, the following ones are common:

More blood goes to your brain, and this may turn your face and ears pink, or give you a pressure headache.

Digestion slows so the blood can flow where it's most needed. Your mouth may get dry, or you might get a stomachache.

Your heart beats harder and faster to bring oxygen-rich blood to your body.

You get butterflies in your stomach because your body is producing chemicals like adrenaline, which boosts your energy.

You get sweaty all over, and your hands may get clammy. Your body produces sweat in anticipation of running or fighting.

The blood rushes to your large muscles (the ones that help you run), decreasing the blood flow in your hands and feet. This makes them feel cooler or cold.

Experts say parents can pass on a tendency to react in an anxious or calm way. Although your genes play a role in your anxiety level, so do other factors. Over the years, you've probably learned to cope with stressful events in certain ways. Maybe you've watched how your mom, dad, or other adults handle stress, and you've learned from them. Or maybe very early on in life you developed your own methods for coping.

It's normal to have some stress in your life—everyone does. And in some ways stress can be good for you. Hard to believe? Think about what it would be like if your school assignments could be turned in on any old date. Or if during athletic events, all the players took as much time as they wanted and never pushed themselves to do their best. What would life be like if no one ever had to set goals, study, take tests, speak before an audience, or perform in any way? Pretty dull, don't you think? Without the extra energy good stress produces, people wouldn't have as much motivation to try new things.

Even positive events—like birthdays, vacations, and special holidays—can cause stress. But again, this kind of stress can feel pretty good, like an adrenaline rush, adding excitement to your life.

However, some stress is definitely negative, and it can become a VERY BIG part of the middle-school years. For example, what if you're dealing with a bully, a divorce in the family, a fight with a friend, poor grades, or some other difficulty? These kinds of problems are tough to handle and can be a huge source of stress. Sometimes you may feel ready to E*X*P*L*O*D*E.

How do you usually deal with negative stress? Maybe you run around outdoors, play with your dog, take a hot shower, or rent a funny video. These are positive ways to cope.

On the other hand, maybe you try to deal with stress in some not-so-positive ways. When you're anxious, do you do too much of the following things?

- eat
- sleep
- skip meals

- watch TV, play video games, or browse online
- stay in your room alone
- put off things you need to do, like homework or chores

It's natural to want to hide or escape when you're feeling stressed out. (Remember your body is ready to fight or *flee*.) If you're spending a lot of time by yourself and withdrawing from people and activities you used to care about, it may be time to get help handling your stress. Talk to an adult you trust and do it today. If an adult isn't available for you right now, you can contact one of the hotlines below.

Boys Town National Hotline
1-800-448-3000
Girls and boys can call this crisis hotline anytime, twenty-four hours a day. You'll talk to a professional counselor who will listen and give you advice on any issue (including stress and other problems). Online, go to: *www.boystown.org.*

Covenant House Nineline
1-800-999-9999
The nineline offers immediate support for young people who need help. You can call twenty-four hours a day, seven days a week. Online, go to: *www.covenanthouse.org.*

Stress is a fact of life. You can't always avoid it, but you *can* manage it. Here are some healthy ways to help yourself cope:

1. **Eat right and exercise.** Eating healthy foods and exercising on a regular basis are important ways to lower your stress level. Physical activity lifts your spirits and helps you feel more relaxed, reducing your stress. Avoid caffeine, a chemical that gives you an energy boost that can temporarily increase your stress level and then make you feel tired afterward. Coffee, tea, and some kinds of soda usually contain caffeine, and so does chocolate.

2. **Get enough sleep.** Studies show that if you're constantly sleep-deprived because you go to bed too late and get up too early, your body will have more trouble handling the stresses of life.

3. **Laugh it up.** Research shows that laughter helps people feel better, happier, and less stressed. Spend time reading funny cartoons, joke books, and humor magazines, or rent a movie starring your favorite comedian.

4. **Have some fun.** Doing something fun can take your mind off your stress. What do you like to do? Who do you enjoy spending time with, and who makes you laugh? Find these people and soak up their positive energy.

5. **Use your problem-solving skills.** Instead of feeling helpless and using your energy to worry about the problem that's causing your stress, figure out the steps you need to take to work things out. Check out pages 102–105 for conflict-resolution tips, and pages 154–157 for help in making decisions.

6. **Do a relaxation exercise.** This kind of exercise involves breathing deeply and imagining a peaceful scene. On the next page is one you can photocopy and do whenever you want to relax. Or you can design one that suits your individual style.

▪▪▪▪▪▪ RELAXATION EXERCISE ▪▪▪▪▪▪

Lie on your bed or in some other comfortable position and place, close your eyes, and imagine a scene that's peaceful and quiet. (A beach with gentle waves lapping at the sand or a hammock swaying beneath a tree, for example.)

Perform the following sequence, beginning at your toes and slowly working your way up your body. If you can get someone to read the instructions to you, you'll find that the exercise is even more relaxing.

- Tense your toes and hold for a count of five. Breathe in deeply and, as you exhale, feel your toes relaxing.

- Keep breathing deeply while you tense your calf muscles. Hold for a count of five. Let go of the tension in those muscles.

- Tense both legs, including your thighs. Keep the tension for a count of five, and then release it.

- Now squeeze your buttocks and your stomach muscles. Hold the tension for a count of five, and then slowly relax those muscles.

- Next, breathe in as you tighten your fingers. Keep the tension in your fingers as you count to five. Relax your hands as you exhale.

- Move on to your arms. Feel both arms tightening up. Count to five and release all the tension.

- Tense your chest while you squeeze your shoulder blades together. Keep the tension for a count of five, and then relax as you exhale.

- Move now to your jaw and cheek muscles, again tensing for five seconds and then releasing the tension.

- Focus on your eyes and forehead, squeezing tightly for five seconds and then feeling all the tension leaving your face.

- Finally, inhale deeply and, as you exhale, imagine any remaining tension leaving your body. How do you feel?

Fighting Invisible Tigers: Stress Management for Teens (Revised & Updated Third Edition) by Earl Hipp (Minneapolis: Free Spirit Publishing Inc., 2008). If you've ever felt overwhelmed, inadequate, tired, or stressed out, you're not alone. This book helps you understand your stress and learn how to deal with it. A "First Aid for Tiger Bites" section offers help for times when you've reached your limit and need fast relief.

FACING YOUR FEARS

Have you ever woken up in the middle of the night frightened by a terrible nightmare? Or maybe you've seen a horror movie that kept you glued to your seat, heart pounding and hands sweating, too scared to move? If so, you know what fear feels like.

You've probably experienced other kinds of fear, too. Fear, like any other emotion, is part of being human. And learning to deal with it is part of growing up.

At this point in your life, you may feel some very common day-to-day fears including:

1. **Being different:** You may be afraid of doing or saying something that other people—particularly the "cool" crowd—will make fun of.

2. **Speaking in public:** Lots of kids feel really nervous when they have to speak in class—even if they know the correct answer. And giving an oral report can be absolute torture for some. A fear of public speaking is also one of the most common fears among adults.

3. **Having something terrible happen:** Maybe you fear losing someone you care about, getting into an accident, or becoming sick. Or maybe you're scared of death. Many adults are fearful about these things, too.

4. **Not doing well in school:** Many students, at some point, get scared about tests, homework, projects, and grades. Some kids live in constant fear of not doing well in school. This fear may particularly affect kids who have learning difficulties.

5. **Having your friends turn against you:** Do you ever get scared your friends will suddenly stop liking you? That they'll find a "better" friend to hang out with? Because friendships are so important during the middle-school years, this kind of fear is common. (Your friends are probably feeling the very same way!)

6. **Not being liked by your teacher:** At the beginning of the school year, some kids are scared their teachers won't like them. Students who feel this way might be worried about succeeding in school, or they may have had problems with a teacher in the past.

7. **Being embarrassed by your family:** This is a prime age for being embarrassed by your family—particularly by your parents who may mean well but tend to say or do things that make you cringe (like reminding you to brush your teeth when your friends are over).

Does this list of fears include the ones that are real to you? Are there others you'd add to it?

Now that you've thought about what you're afraid of, what can you do to face your fears? Plenty! Here are some suggestions:

▨   **Look at the feelings *behind* the fear.** Suppose you're afraid your best friend will dump you to get in with the "popular" group. Ask yourself: *What is my fear based on? What else am I feeling?* Are you worried you and your friend don't really share the same interests anymore? Do you feel you're not as cool or as much fun as other people? Do you think your friend is changing in ways you're not? Chances are, you're feeling more than fear.

▨   **Ask yourself if the fear is *realistic.*** In other words, is it likely to happen or not? Using the example above, think about whether it's realistic that your friend might desert you. Has your friend done anything like that in the past? Is your friend ignoring you or showing any other signs of abandoning you? If not, the fear probably isn't realistic.

- **Talk to your mom or dad, or another adult you trust.** If you keep your fears locked inside, they may start to seem much bigger than they really are. An adult may be able to help you figure out what your fear is based on and whether it's realistic or not.

- **Face it!** Once you've identified your fear and you understand it a little better, you can face it head on. Start by making a step-by-step plan of action. You can track your progress using a chart similar to the one below. Decide what small step you can take first, and then figure out the next bigger step to follow. Determine what further steps to take from there.

My fear: I'm afraid to do the big class presentation that's required next month.

What it's based on: If I look and act nervous, everyone will know I am. I want to be accepted. I want people to think I'm more confident than I really am.

	Action	When Taken	How Did I feel Afterward?
Step 1:	Raise my hand during class and ask questions.	Tuesday in social studies class. Thursday during science.	Relieved I did it.
Step 2:	Start practicing my report out loud at home.	Three times this week.	A little more confident each time.
Step 3:	Rehearse part of my report in front of my family.	Saturday evening after dinner.	Excited—they said it was good!

Tackling fears isn't easy, so you'll have to be patient with yourself. You may have to do one or more steps over again, until your fear lessens. Ask for help from friends, family members, or trusted adults in designing a plan and supporting you as you carry it out.

DEALING WITH ANGER

How do you know when someone's angry? Some people scream and yell, and it's obvious they're upset. But others get very quiet and may even refuse to speak. And still others show their anger in hidden ways. They may spread rumors about the person they're mad at or plot revenge. Anger is a powerful but confusing emotion. Whether it comes on suddenly or slowly builds inside you, anger can make you feel out of control.

Suppose you get mad at your parents—how do you act? Do you yell, scream, slam doors, throw things, or storm into your room? Maybe you stop speaking to them? Each person has his or her own anger style. Yours may be very similar to your mom's or dad's, or very different.

Getting mad once in a while is okay; anger is part of being human. If you're angry, it helps to release your feelings instead of bottling them inside. Shouting at people doesn't work, though, and neither does acting out in violence. What does work? Dealing with anger positively. Sound impossible? It's not! Here are some tips for resolving anger in healthy ways:

1. **Do something physical.** Anger produces a lot of extra energy in your body. It makes you feel like you want to yell or even use your fists. If you're so mad you can barely think straight, run around outside, jump rope, practice karate kicks, go skateboarding, or turn up the volume and dance like crazy in your room.

2. **Take a moment to calm down.** It might not always be possible to do something physical, especially if you're in class or in the car. What can you do then? Calm down by closing your eyes and taking a long, slow, deep breath through your nose, slowly counting to five. Then breathe out through your nose, slowly counting backwards from five. Repeat this a few times until you feel more peaceful.

3. **Tell yourself not to let anger get the best of you.** Sometimes people don't even know they've done something to anger you. For example, maybe someone accidentally bumps you while you're carrying your lunch tray, causing your drink to spill. Is that going to ruin your day? You can choose to put your anger behind you and move on. Get your mind off your anger by thinking about something positive.

4. **Express your anger.** Like other feelings, anger needs to be expressed. You can write about your emotions or talk to a friend or an adult face-to-face.

5. **Tell the person you're angry with how you feel.** You may feel uncomfortable telling someone you're angry, but it's worth it. Or you may feel that it's easier to ignore the issue or stop speaking to the person, but do you know what happens if you do? The anger stays with you, even if it's buried deep inside.

Straight Talk About Anger by Christine Dentemaro and Rachel Kranz (New York: Facts On File, 1995). Everyone gets angry sometimes, and this book offers lots of advice on how to deal with anger—your own and someone else's. You'll find information on the causes of anger and tips on dealing with it in healthy, positive ways.

SADNESS AND GRIEF

When you're sad, you might feel like your heart is broken or empty, or you just can't cope with what's going on. Unfortunately, sad things happen in life, and everyone experiences hurt and disappointment. Events like divorce, moving, a family illness, or changing schools can all cause sadness. So can losing a pet you love.

Sadness, like other emotions, eventually passes. But knowing this may not be a comfort when you're sad. One way to release sadness is through tears. Crying is your body's way of letting out painful feelings.

"One of my classmates, Jeremy, drowned when he was ten. When my mom told me, I was very sad. While I cried, she comforted me. At first, I couldn't believe he had died. Jeremy was very nice and very smart. Everyone liked him. I still think about him sometimes. Last summer, my archery camp counselor died. She was only about nineteen and died very suddenly of a brain aneurysm. I was glad that I'd gotten to know her. It's scary to know people can die when they're young."

LIZ, 11

When you were younger, you cried often to express your feelings and needs. Now that you're older, you're probably more self-conscious about letting people see your tears. If you're a boy, you may have gotten the message "Boys don't cry." And whether you're a boy or girl, you may think crying isn't mature. Actually, crying is a healthy way to let out your feelings. You may cry if you feel sad or angry, or even if you're watching a sentimental movie. No one is ever too grown-up to shed some tears.

You can handle sadness in many other ways as well. Talk to someone who can give you support—a friend, parent, teacher, or school counselor. Express your feelings in your journal, too, or through music, art, or poetry. Get outdoors to exercise and breathe some fresh air. Sometimes what you need most is a hug or a shoulder to cry on—don't be afraid to reach out to someone you love.

One of the saddest times of all is when somebody you feel close to dies—perhaps a grandparent or another family member, a friend or a friend's parent, or a classmate or teacher at school. At first, you may not even believe something so terrible has happened because the pain of the loss is almost unbearable. Or you may be so upset that your emotions shut down. Everybody grieves differently. The important thing is to talk to someone about what you're going through.

Many kids have their first experience with death during the middle-school years, be it the loss of a pet or a person they love. The result is a tangle of emotions—sadness, grief, confusion, guilt, anger, and even fear. If you've lost a loved one or someone else who was important to you, it's normal to start questioning why life is so unfair or why people have to die. You may have lots of questions that are too big to answer on your own. Find out how you can talk with a religious advisor, a counselor, or someone else who's trained to help people deal with their sadness. You don't have to go through the pain of loss totally alone.

Sometimes kids experience a sadness that doesn't seem to be related to a specific event. If you're unhappy and the feeling hangs on for a long time, you might be depressed. Young people can get depression, just like adults. Some signs of depression may include:

- feeling helpless or hopeless
- having trouble sleeping through the night or feeling tired all the time
- a sadness that goes on and on
- feeling very angry with yourself or others
- being excessively anxious

If this sounds like what you're going through, get help *right away*. Talk to a trusted adult or look in your Yellow Pages under "Crisis Hotlines." You can also call one of the hotline numbers listed on page 60.

When Nothing Matters Anymore: A Survival Guide for Depressed Teens (Revised & Updated Edition) by Bev Cobain, R.N.,C. (Minneapolis: Free Spirit Publishing Inc., 2007). Are you feeling helpless, sad, lonely, angry, or unhappy? This book can help you figure out if you're depressed. First-person stories about young people with depression let you know you're not alone and you can find the help you need.

Internet Mental Health
www.mentalhealth.com
This Web site offers information about all aspects of mental health and places to turn for professional help.

HELPING FRIENDS WITH THEIR FEELINGS

Your friends may be going through many of the same changes you are, physical and emotional. And, at times, your friends may feel confused or stressed. What can you do to help? Be a friend. Above all, that means being a caring and trustworthy listener.

If your friends ask for advice, you can give it. Otherwise, just listen and let them know you care. What else can you do? Suggest they talk to a parent or school counselor to get some help. You can also give your friends hotline numbers or the names of organizations that deal with the kinds of problems your friends are facing. You can even suggest calling the hotlines or organizations together.

If a friend tells you something secret or private, what should you do? It depends on the situation. Friends need to be able to trust each other. That's just a basic rule of friendship. So if a friend tells you a secret, it's a good idea to keep it to yourself. Otherwise, you could lose your friend's trust—or even the friendship.

However, if a friend tells you something private *but is in danger* (for example, he or she is being abused, has an eating disorder, is suicidal, or is depressed), get help from an adult right away. These are the kinds of problems that are too serious to handle alone—no matter how smart you are or how much you care. Getting adult help for a friend who needs it is NOT a break in trust! It's the best thing you can do for both of you.

At this time in your life, you no longer think of yourself as a child. You're more mature and better able to handle your problems on your own. You probably want other people to see you as grown-up and capable of taking care of yourself. As a result, you might sometimes be tempted to hide your emotions or pretend you're feeling fine when you're not. Want to know a real sign of growing up? Learning how to talk about your feelings honestly and express them in healthy ways.

SURVIVAL TIP #4

CONNECT WITH YOUR FAMILY

Have you felt different around your parents* lately? Maybe their choice of music seems strange, or they do embarrassing things like kiss you in front of your friends. It's not necessarily your *parents* who are different. Because you're changing as you grow up, your relationships with the people you love are changing, too.

Although you still need your parents, you're more independent now. As you pull away, they might try to pull you closer or have a hard time letting go. Sometimes your relationship with them might feel like a tug-of-war. You may be pulling at different ends of the same rope, but you're still connected. That's what survival tip #4 is all about: staying connected!

*We know that kids live in many different situations. When we say "parents," we mean the adult or adults primarily responsible for you.

DOES IT FEEL LIKE YOU'RE TALKING TO A BRICK WALL?

Have you ever had a conversation that went sort of like this?

KiD: "Mom, I need a calculator for my math test tomorrow."

MOM (WHiLE PAYiNG BiLLS): "Just a minute."

KiD: "It's important! I need to put it in my backpack now, so I won't forget it."

MOM: "I'll be done in just a second."

KiD: "You're not listening to me!"

MOM: "Okay fine." (stopping her work) "Now, what did you say?"

KiD: "Never mind, I'll just fail my test tomorrow."

MOM: "You hardly gave me a chance to answer you!"

Communication between parents and kids often becomes more difficult during the middle-school years. That's because you've entered a new stage of development. You now have more opinions and ideas, and different needs. You probably want to be part of adult conversations and family decisions—because you're older and you'd like your voice to be heard.

Adolescence is the time when you begin to establish your own interests, and your likes and dislikes. That's part of figuring out who you are (your identity). You may also be discovering ways you're different from your parents. Conflict with your family is the inevitable result of working on your own identity.

Although you love your parents, you may now have doubts about their rules and how they run things at home. It's normal for parents and kids to disagree sometimes. But in some families with middle-school age kids, arguments happen often and ordinary conversations can turn into battles. Family members may say hurtful words or have trouble talking. Communication problems make it hard to get along.

To make matters more difficult, you're at an age when you aren't as comfortable showing affection for your parents. They may see this as a sign that you don't care about them or need them as much as you once did. (Even if you don't really feel that way.)

Communicating openly, honestly, and respectfully is one key to strengthening family bonds and resolving conflicts. Here are some communication tips to try:

- **Use "I messages."** These are statements that rely on the word *I* to communicate. For example, "I feel angry when I get yelled at" or "I feel like you sometimes treat me like a child, and I want to show you how responsible I can be." Instead of placing blame on the other person, "I messages" focus on feelings and help defuse tense situations.

- **Don't scream or yell.** Talking calmly and politely shows respect for your family and gives you a better chance of being heard. If you get nasty, your parents will probably react to your tone of voice rather than to what you're saying. Show respect to get respect.

- **Say what you mean in a direct way.** Gather up your courage, and then make your point or ask your question. If you're worried about hurting someone's feelings or not getting the answer you want, remember that "I messages" are a helpful way to communicate. Try again, using *I* to start off each sentence.

- **Be aware of what others feel.** Everyone has a point of view—let each person have a say. Suppose your parents make a rule about not hanging out with your friends on school nights. Consider your parents' point of view: maybe they think you won't get your homework done if you're spending time with friends. Show them that you understand this, and they'll be more likely to listen to your side of the story.

- **Be open to a little give and take.** One way to solve a problem is by compromising, meaning each person *gives* a little to *get* a little. Using the above example, what could you do to compromise? Suppose you make sure your homework is done before you go out with your friends, and you agree to be home before 8 P.M.? That may be a solution everyone can agree on.

- **Watch your body language.** Body language is a way of communicating without words. Suppose you yell at your dad, and he asks for an apology. You say you're sorry, but you've got your arms crossed, you're scowling, or your eyes are rolling. What your dad "hears" is, "I'm not a bit sorry!" Be aware of your facial expressions and your pose. Also, try to make eye contact, so the other person knows you're paying attention.

- **Learn to listen.** During a disagreement or conversation, people sometimes tune each other out. Or they focus on what they're going to say next. Learning to listen takes some practice and patience. But other people feel like they're being treated with respect when they know you're really listening—and that makes them more likely to listen to you.

> "One of the problems in my family is that my dad doesn't seem to ever listen; he always seems kind of preoccupied. And my brother, Keith, is moody and has a lot of annoying habits. When we're talking as a family, Keith always wants it to be about himself and he makes sure the attention is all on him. I feel like no one notices me!"
>
> **JULIE, 12**

Do you feel that your family needs some help communicating? These books contain tips for better communication.

Get a Clue! A Parents' Guide to Understanding and Communicating with Your Preteen by Ellen Rosenberg (New York: Henry Holt and Company, 1999). In this book, kids ages eight to fourteen share their suggestions on how parents can better communicate with their children about self-esteem, feelings, getting along, and other important topics.

The Tween Years: A Parent's Guide for Surviving Those Terrific, Turbulent, and Trying Times Between Childhood and Adolescence by Donna G. Corwin (Chicago, IL: Contemporary Books, 1999). This guide to understanding kids ages ten to thirteen includes lots of advice about communication and parent-child conflicts.

FAMILY HOT BUTTONS

What are the hot issues in your home? Here are a few typical ones in families with middle-school age kids:

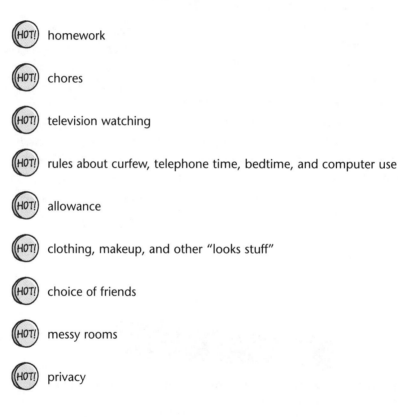

(HOT!) homework

(HOT!) chores

(HOT!) television watching

(HOT!) rules about curfew, telephone time, bedtime, and computer use

(HOT!) allowance

(HOT!) clothing, makeup, and other "looks stuff"

(HOT!) choice of friends

(HOT!) messy rooms

(HOT!) privacy

What hot buttons would you add to the list? Family hot buttons are part of the tug-of-war between you and your parents. You want to be treated as a grown-up; they want you to act more grown-up. So, in a way, you've got the same goal in mind. Hot button issues are conflicts over what being grown-up really means. You want more *freedom*. Your parents want you to be more RESPONSIBLE.

Because you're not yet an adult, your parents still have control over many parts of your life. At the same time, you're growing up, and you're better able to make decisions now. You're old enough to choose what activities to pursue, what to wear, who you spend time with, what you do on weekends, and more. But your parents still want to have their say—and they may say *a lot* about your choices of clothing, friends, and activities. That's because, more than anything, they want what's best for you.

But sometimes your parents' concern might feel stifling—just when you want more freedom to explore the world and discover your place in it. Do you want to know the best way to get more freedom? Be responsible! If you'd like to be able to do more—stay up later, go places with friends, spend some of your money on whatever you want—then you've got to prove to your parents that you can handle your freedom.

Suppose your parents drop you off at the mall to spend time with your friends. They're trusting you to be responsible. What happens if, a few hours later, your parents return to pick you up and you're nowhere to be found? Or what if you decide to go to a friend's house after school, and you forget to call home first? If you break their trust, your parents might believe you can't handle freedom *or* responsibility. The result? They may limit you even more. But if you're on time or you remember to call, your parents will know you can handle your greater freedom and probably will reward you with more.

> "Really great parents give you just enough freedom and responsibility—not too much, not too little. Plus, you can talk to them and share your emotions."
>
> **JESSE, 14**

Rules, Rules, and More Rules

Do you have lots of rules at your house? Like:

- No TV until homework's done.
- Be in bed by 10:00.
- Take turns sharing the computer.
- Phone calls can't last more than twenty minutes.

While rules don't necessarily make life fun, they *do* help keep the peace. You have rules to follow at home, at school, and in your community. Without rules, life would be very confusing and messy.

Think about some of your family's household rules. Are they helpful? Are they fair? How do they ensure that your home functions smoothly? Who makes the rules? Are there any rules you'd change if you could? You may want to talk to your parents about some of these issues.

Many household rules have to do with chores. Have you ever met someone—kid or adult—who actually *enjoys* doing chores around the house? On the other hand, do you know anyone who likes eating at a sticky table covered in old pancake syrup? Or enjoys spending a half hour looking for a favorite T-shirt, only to find it's still in the laundry hamper, complete with a chocolate stain that looks like it won't ever come out?

Think about the chores that need to be done at your home. Is everyone doing a fair share of the work? To find out, use the chart on the next page. It can help you track many of the tasks that families have to complete each day.

DIRECTIONS: Photocopy the Chore Chart on the next page. Over the next week, fill it in. Write who completes each chore (you can list more than one person) and how much time it takes. Give each chore a "difficulty rating," using a scale of 1–3. (1 means it's easy, 2 means it takes more effort, and 3 means it's hard.)

At the end of the week, add up all the hours each person spends on household tasks. Who does the most? Who does the least? Which family members are responsible for most of the difficult work? Is there a way to help lighten their loads?

CHORE CHART

	WHO MAINLY DOES IT?	APPROXIMATE TIME IT TAKES EACH WEEK	DIFFICULTY RATING
Prepare meals			
Set the table			
Clear the table after meals			
Wash dishes or load dishwasher			
Put clean dishes away			
Take out garbage			
Vacuum			
Dust			
Do laundry			
Iron			
Clean up clutter			
Scrub bathrooms			
Shop for groceries			
Make lunches			
Do yard work			
Take care of pets			
Make beds			
Other?			
Other?			

Are the household chores divided fairly in your home? Are you doing your part? Are you doing too much, making it more difficult for you to keep up with your homework and after-school activities? Think about ways to make some changes and talk to your parents about your ideas.

When everyone pitches in at home, a household runs more smoothly. Family members then have more time to relax or enjoy themselves—and that means fewer disagreements about chores. Added bonus: Your parents will notice how *responsible* it was of you to help organize the household routine!

The TV "Wars"

Television is a source of conflict in many families today. Does your family watch a lot of TV? Research shows that most people underestimate how much they watch. TV viewing can be hypnotizing. You turn the television on, and soon two hours have gone by.

Why is it that parents who enjoy relaxing in front of the TV don't like to see their kids do the same? Probably because these parents know they watch too much TV themselves, and that a lot of what's on television is mindless or violent. They also know there are more relaxing, productive, and fun things to do than watch television. Watching TV is a habit for many people—often a very time-consuming one. Television isn't necessarily bad; many programs are funny, entertaining, or informative. The trouble begins when the TV habit gets out of hand.

Try tracking how much television you watch in a week. Figure out when you watch it most, what kind of mood you're in when you start, and how you feel when you turn it off. Before you begin this exercise, make a prediction about how much TV you watch. You may be surprised at what you find out afterward!

DIRECTIONS: Photocopy the TV log on the following pages. Each night before bed, fill it in. After a week, add up all your TV hours.

TV LOG

For the week of _____

MONDAY

I turned the TV on at _____ (time)

I turned it off at _____ (time)

Before I started, I felt _____

Afterward I felt _____

Total hours spent watching TV today _____

TUESDAY

I turned the TV on at _____ (time)

I turned it off at _____ (time)

Before I started, I felt _____

Afterward I felt _____

Total hours spent watching TV today _____

WEDNESDAY

I turned the TV on at _____ (time)

I turned it off at _____ (time)

Before I started, I felt _____

Afterward I felt _____

Total hours spent watching TV today _____

THURSDAY

I turned the TV on at _____ (time)

I turned it off at _____ (time)

Before I started, I felt _____

Afterward I felt _____

Total hours spent watching TV today _____

Continued on next page ⟶

TV LOG

(CONTINUED)

FRIDAY

I turned the TV on at _____ (time)

I turned it off at _____ (time)

Before I started, I felt _____

Afterward I felt _____

Total hours spent watching TV today _____

SATURDAY

I turned the TV on at _____ (time)

I turned it off at _____ (time)

Before I started, I felt _____

Afterward I felt _____

Total hours spent watching TV today _____

SUNDAY

I turned the TV on at _____ (time)

I turned it off at _____ (time)

Before I started, I felt _____

Afterward I felt _____

Total hours spent watching TV today _____

TOTAL HOURS SPENT WATCHING TELEVISION THIS WEEK _____

Now that you've logged your TV time for a week, what did you find out about yourself? Did you spend more or less time watching TV than you expected? Did television improve your mood or not?

If you think you watched too much TV, make a list of activities you could have been doing instead. Here are some sample ideas:

- reading a book, magazine, or newspaper
- riding your bike or doing another outdoor activity
- starting a new hobby
- playing a board game or working on a puzzle
- sketching with colored pencils
- writing in a journal
- calling a friend or sending email
- catching up on homework
- daydreaming

If you want to watch less television each week, decide which shows you can live without. Make a plan to do something else while these programs are on. (Refer to your activities list for ideas.) Also, make an effort to keep the TV off while you're doing chores, hobbies, or homework.

If you'd like, share the TV log with your family. Find out if they're watching too much television and if they'd like to find other fun things to do instead. It's fine if families sometimes spend their free time together watching TV or renting movies, but there are other cool activities to try, too. Maybe your family would enjoy going on a picnic or hike, making a meal together, going to the library, taking a walk, playing a game of touch football, or just talking. There's a lot you can do when you turn off the TV and tune in to each other!

Privacy

Do you spend a lot of time alone in your room or some other place doing homework, trying on clothes, talking on the phone, listening to music, or working on your hobby? It feels good to be alone sometimes, day-dreaming and pursuing your interests. Everybody needs private time.

Do your parents respect your privacy? Do you respect theirs? How about your brothers or sisters (if you have any): do they understand that you need to be alone sometimes? Do they borrow your stuff without asking or get into your personal things like your private notes or email?

Privacy is a major issue during the middle-school years. At this stage of your life, you need your own space. That's part of the struggle for independence. It can feel like a really big deal if someone invades your privacy.

Some family members may borrow your stuff and forget to put it back, barge in while you're in the bathroom, or come into your room without knocking. You may feel annoyed when things like this happen, but the truth is, you'd probably miss your family very much if they suddenly disappeared from your life.

If you need a little more space, talk to your parents about making a privacy contract. Let them know you still enjoy being with the family but you need private time, too. You can create the contract yourself (using the form on the next page) or ask everyone in the family to work on one together. Have each family member sign it, and then make photocopies everyone can keep.

PRIVACY CONTRACT

We, _____ , agree to
(each person's name goes here)

respect the privacy of everyone in this family.

The purpose of this contract is to remind us that

each family member has a need for private time.

This contract is also about respecting each other's

personal belongings. When we sign this form, we

agree to treat each other and each person's

belongings with respect. We also agree that it's

okay to have some time alone. If we want private

time, we will let other people know in a polite way.

Signed _____

Agreements and Disagreements

What can you do when you and your parents just can't agree? You could agree to disagree, but this is easier said than done. Or you could work together to come up with a compromise everyone can live with.

For example, maybe you've recently had some disagreements about your allowance. Have a respectful conversation about it and figure out why you disagree. Here's an example of how to bring up the issue:

YOU: "Dad, can we talk about my allowance? Lately, I've been finding that I don't have enough money to get through the week. I think I should get a little more than you're giving me."

DAD: "I think your allowance is high enough. Sometimes you don't even do the chores you're supposed to do."

YOU: "I know. If I promise to finish my chores, could you raise my allowance?"

DAD: "How do I know you're really going to get them done?"

YOU: "Give me a chance to prove it to you. In two weeks, if I'm not doing better, you can keep the amount of my allowance the same."

DAD: "Sounds good. You know, I'd even be willing to give you a little extra money for extra chores."

YOU: "Great! Now, let's put it in writing."

Write the agreement on two pieces of paper, so each person has a copy. If you put the agreement someplace where you'll see it each day, you'll be more likely to remember what you've said you'll do. It's not enough to simply *make* a promise, you've got to *keep* it, too.

After you've made the first agreement and stuck to it for a month or so, it will feel like part of your normal routine. Most likely, you'll find that you and your parents have stopped arguing about the issue. At that point, you can decide if you're ready to make a new agreement. Go back to the list of hot buttons (see page 76) to see which one is causing conflict.

Suppose you and your parents have been arguing about how messy your room is. Maybe you're content living with clutter on every surface and a laundry pile a mile high. Talk to your parents about the situation. Can both sides agree to give a little, so you can put the argument to rest? Maybe you could come up with an agreement like this:

You agree to:
- make your bed every day before school
- empty your trash can at least once a week
- keep clean clothes off the floor

Your parents agree to:
- stop criticizing your room
- refrain from reminding you to clean up
- shut the door if they can't stand the clutter

What happens if someone breaks an agreement you've made together? Decide ahead of time what the consequences will be. That way, everyone knows what to expect.

If you're the one who breaks the agreement, admit what you've done and apologize. Taking responsibility for your actions shows maturity. If your mom or dad slips up, talk about it. Explain how you feel about the broken agreement. And be forgiving. After all, parents are human, and they make mistakes, too.

Family Meetings and Why They Help

A great time to bring up agreements—and disagreements—is during a family meeting. Here's what you can do to make family meetings work for you:

1. **Name the time and place.** Decide *how often* you'll meet (once a month, once a week, whenever a big issue comes up), *what time* (after dinner, after homework), and *where* (the kitchen, the living room). You can also set a time limit for the meetings, so they don't drag on too long.

2. **Set up some ground rules.** Important rules include listening respectfully, not interrupting each other, and being sure not to tease, whine, or raise voices.

3. **Decide on a way to begin each meeting.** Start each meeting on a positive note, even if you've gathered to discuss a conflict. Some families begin by letting each person talk about his or her day: What was the best thing that happened? Were there any surprises?

4. **Take turns talking.** Some families pass around a "talking stick" for the person who's speaking to hold. You can use anything for a talking stick. If you'd like, make one for your family. Start with a wooden spoon and add paint or decorations. Whoever is holding the talking stick gets to speak without being interrupted.

5. **Determine how the meetings will be run.** Who will be the leader (or whatever title your family decides to give for this role)? How often will the

roles change—every week, every month? Will each family member get an opportunity to lead a meeting?

6. **Decide how to handle the issues that come up.** Does someone need to apologize? Do agreements need to be made? Make an effort to resolve the issues in each meeting. Don't give up!

7. **Come up with a way to end the meetings.** Go for something upbeat. For example, create a fun slogan to end every meeting. Other ideas include having each person say one positive thing about another family member or express one thing they're grateful for.

It's helpful to have a regular time and place to share thoughts, opinions, or misunderstandings—and to talk about solutions. These meetings are a positive step in building a healthy relationship with your family and bringing everyone a little closer.

The How Rude! Handbook of Family Manners for Teens by Alex J. Packer, Ph.D. (Minneapolis: Free Spirit Publishing Inc., 2004). This entertaining yet informative book covers the basics of creating a civilized home—a place where people talk instead of yell, pick up after themselves, respect each other, fight fair, and don't hog the bathroom.

DEALING WITH DIVORCE

Good communication and family meetings can solve or prevent many family problems. But these tools aren't enough for every family situation. Some family problems are too big or serious for those solutions. What kind of problems? The ones every kid hopes to avoid—like parents who fight a lot, separate, or get divorced. You might know about situations like these if a friend has gone through them, or if they're part of your own life.

During the middle-school years, many kids experience divorce in their families. If your parents have recently split up or you're adjusting to a new stepfamily, you may be feeling painful emotions like anger, guilt, or sadness. It may help to know that you aren't to blame for the break-up. Parents divorce each other—not you.

How you react to your parents' divorce will depend, in part, on how they're handling it. The first year is often the hardest, but as time goes by, the situation usually gets easier. If your parents spend a lot of time complaining about each other to you, you're not betraying either one if you listen. If the conversations upset you, talk to your parents about your feelings. It may also be helpful to talk to a friend, especially one who has gone through a similar situation.

Who else can you turn to when, for whatever reason, your parents aren't there for you and you need to talk? On pages 53–54, you'll find information about reaching out to trusted adults. You can look for these adults in your *extended family* (aunts, uncles, or other relatives), at *school* (a teacher, coach, school psychologist, guidance counselor, or social worker), or through your *place of worship* (a religious advisor or youth group leader). Sometimes you might feel awkward about sharing family problems because the conflicts are so personal. But keeping problems locked inside you to protect your family's privacy only hurts you more.

THE SIBLING SCENE

A thirteen-year-old we know told us, "Great sibling is an oxymoron." An oxymoron is a contradiction. Do *you* agree there's no such thing as a great sibling?

If you have a brother or sister, you already know that sibling rivalry is a natural fact of life. No siblings get along *all* the time. Think about how often you fight with your sister or brother compared to how much of the time you actually enjoy the relationship. Are the good times and bad times balanced?

What do you and your sibling usually disagree about? Do you dislike sharing your stuff? Are you in competition with each other? Does one of you sometimes feel jealous of the other one? Do you fight about chores?

This may come as a surprise, but when you and your sibling argue about who gets to sit in the most comfortable chair, who deserves the bigger piece of dessert, who has more pairs of jeans, and all the other things siblings fight over, what you're *really* in conflict about is attention and love from your parents.

As soon as there were two of you, you and your brother or sister probably started keeping careful records of who got more or less at any given time—without even realizing it. In fact, every time either one of you said, "Mom, no fair that he got more than me!" or "Dad, watch *ME* now!" what you were really saying was, "Show me you love me, too!" This is true whether you're the firstborn, a middle child, or the youngest in the family. All kids with siblings have, at some point, felt worried about getting their fair share of love and attention—even if they know that their parents care deeply about all of them.

One thing to remember is that having a brother or sister is like having a special gift. Siblings can be great listeners, advice-givers, and secret-keepers. But only if you've got a strong relationship based on love and respect.

Whether your sibling relationship is good or not-so-good, you can do something to improve it. Here are some ideas:

- **Every day, do one thing (big or small) to show love for a brother or sister.** Offer a kind word, a compliment, or some help with a chore or homework.

- **Once a week, spend time together playing a game both of you like.** This is a healthy way to compete with each other—and have fun at the same time.

- **Confide in each other.** You may get along well with your parents, but perhaps they don't always understand the things that are important to someone your age. It helps to talk to a sister or brother. Remember, though, secrets need to be kept private. If you tell each other's secrets, you won't be able to trust each other again. (An exception to this rule is if you're worried about your sibling, and you need to go to a parent for help.)

- **Ask for advice and give it in return.** This is one of the nicest things siblings can do for each other—especially since you know and understand each other so well!

- **If you have younger sisters or brothers, think of ways they can help you.** Little kids love to be of help and feel included. If you want help with a chore, ask your younger brother or sister to pitch in. If you've misplaced something, chances are your younger sibling can find it by crawling under the bed or looking in other places you might not think of. Come up with other creative ways to get a sibling's help—and remember to lend a hand in return.

- **If you have older sisters or brothers, think of ways they can help you.** Your older siblings probably know a little bit more about life since they've lived longer than you. Talk to them about mistakes they've made or lessons they've learned. Find out what middle school was like for them.

- **Make each other laugh.** Tell each other jokes and riddles. Rent a funny movie together. Play a game of charades. Practice your best imitations in front of each other. Whatever gets you laughing!

STAYING CLOSE TO YOUR FAMILY

Do you feel close to your family—even when you're physically far apart (for example, if one of your parents is traveling or if you're away at camp)? What about when you feel "far apart" in the sense of your ideas or opinions—are you still close to your family even when you disagree? If the answer to these questions is yes, this suggests your family has strong and lasting ties.

What if you don't feel as close to your family as you'd like? Try to figure out what's making it difficult to connect. Set up a family meeting, so all members can express their points of view. Then take steps to solve the issues that come up.

Families can strengthen their connections in other ways, too. If you want to build family togetherness, here's how to get started:

1. **Have a family night.** You can have family night once a week, once a month, or whenever you want. Choose a night and mark it on the calendar so everyone remembers. That can be your evening to cook a meal together, order take-out food, see a movie, attend a sporting event, play a board game, or do anything else your family enjoys.

2. **Volunteer together.** Volunteering your time and energy will help you feel good about yourselves *and* the people (or animals) you're helping. Plus, this is a great way to spend time together! You can serve food at a soup kitchen, clean up litter in your community, or walk dogs at a local animal shelter. Explore volunteering options that are available within your community or through your place of worship.

3. **Put your creativity to work—as a team.** Have you ever considered making your own family newspaper or newsletter? Every family member can contribute their unique talents—articles, cartoons, editorials, movie reviews, an advice column, or interviews. If you've got some computer know-how, you can make the written pieces look like those in a real newspaper. Another idea is to work on family photo albums together, so you can relive memories while creating a lasting project everyone can enjoy.

4. **Plan a family vacation.** A vacation doesn't have to be far away or expensive to be fun. How about camping? Or taking a long weekend to explore sights in your community or state? Or what about a vacation in your own home? If you'd like to travel during vacation, perhaps everyone in the family can work together to save extra money.

5. **Create new family traditions.** How does your family celebrate Thanksgiving? Valentine's Day? The New Year? What about Christmas, Hanukkah, Kwanzaa, or other religious occasions? Each family observes

holidays in its own unique way, and these events can be a special time of celebration and family closeness. Think about your family's traditions: do you honor them each year? Find new ways to personalize the holidays, while maintaining your old traditions. For example, you might create one-of-a-kind decorations or give each other handmade gifts.

6. **Make a family shadow box.** Families are so busy that it's hard to remember the fun things that happen during the year. One way to keep the memories from fading is to make a family shadow box. Set aside one evening for the project. You'll need a three-dimensional plastic frame (you can find one at most stores that sell frames or craft materials), glue, and mementos from each family member, such as photos, ticket stubs, pressed plants, or favorite sayings. Arrange the items together in an artistic way, glue them to the back of the frame, and display the creation where the whole family can enjoy it.

7. **Keep in touch with relatives.** Is there one person in your family who sends all the birthday cards or letters to relatives? Why not give that person a hand? You can also keep in touch with relatives on your own by sending notes, email, or jokes and riddles. A fun family project is to make a video-tape or an audio cassette tape to mail to faraway family members. Be sure to keep a copy for your home.

■ ▨ ▨ ▨

The middle-school years are a time when you're becoming more independent, but your family is still an important connection for you. In a way, you're kind of like a boat going out to sea: there's plenty of fun and adventure ahead, but isn't it a little bit comforting to know that, not too far in the distance, there's a shore you can head to when the seas get rough?

Family life isn't always smooth sailing, as you probably know. But a strong family relationship can be one of your greatest sources of support—now and always.

FIND, MAKE, AND

KEEP FRIENDS

You've probably always had friends—the kids on your street, in your class, or in your community. But in middle school, friendships deepen, and you connect with people your own age more than you ever have before. At this stage of your life, it's natural to get closer to your friends, talk with them on the phone a lot, and spend more time hanging out with them after school and on weekends.

The middle-school years are a time when kids often form tighter groups or cliques. Some of the people you've always thought of as friends may decide to hang out with a new group, perhaps one that doesn't make you feel welcome. Or you might start at a new school, where you're looking at a lot of new faces in class and at lunch. These situations can be intimidating, and that's where survival tip #5 comes in. It's all about finding, making, and keeping good friends—skills that can help you now and for the rest of your life.

It's also about another important part of middle-school social life, and that's *romance*. Maybe it's the last thing on your mind, or maybe you've already had lots of crushes—perhaps you're somewhere in-between. No matter what your attitude and experiences have been so far, you may be very interested in learning a little more about love.

WHAT'S FRIENDSHIP ALL ABOUT?

When you were younger, you probably made friends with kids in your neighborhood. But now you're older, and many things in your life have changed. You've got new interests and activities, and more freedom to do what you like to do. At school, you may change rooms to attend different classes, instead of staying in the same room all day long. You're probably meeting more kids now, which gives you lots of opportunities to make friends.

> "A friend is someone who's kind, lets you talk, stands up for you—and shares lunch with you when you've forgotten yours."
>
> BRIANNA, 12

Finding friends means getting to know new people. If you're naturally kind of shy, you may find it harder to make friends. As difficult as it may be at first, you'll find that building friendships gets easier with practice.

What's the most important thing you can do when making friends? Be yourself. Sometimes, you may feel that you need to put on an act to get people interested in you or make them think you're cool. But putting on an act can be very tiring. Real friends like you because of who you are—for your personality, values, and strengths. You don't have to be phony with real friends.

Here are some more tips for making friends:

1. **Get out and about.** A friend isn't going to magically show up at your door! Find out what's going on in your neighborhood and community. Is there a sports team you can join? A local recreation center you can check out? Maybe a community-sponsored club? What do kids nearby do for fun?

2. **Join in at school.** Participating in an after-school activity is a great way to get to know people. What are your interests—drama, writing, art, athletics, community service, computers, music? Plenty of activities are available in middle school. Figure out what you like to do, and then get involved.

3. **Be friendly at school.** You may be surprised at how quickly other people respond to a smile or friendly hello. To break the ice, you could ask someone for the homework assignment or say something about a teacher or

class. After the other person responds, try to get a conversation going. Ask questions and act interested. Most people like to talk about themselves and appreciate it when someone listens.

How can you tell if someone is a potential friend? You'll feel a connection to the person. Maybe you have a lot in common—you like the same jokes or activities. Sometimes you and your friend might be very different—one of you may be more athletic, and the other more social. But you admire each other's positive qualities, and together, you complement each other.

Once you've got one friend, you'll feel stronger and more secure. Then you'll be ready to make more friends. If there's someone at school you're interested in getting to know, invite that person to do something fun. Rent a movie, shoot some hoops, or just sit together at lunch. Have a party and invite people you'd like to get to know better. Soon enough, you'll receive invitations in return.

Fun Things to Do with Friends

What do you like to do with your friends? Maybe you spend a lot of time hanging out, using the computer, playing video games, or just talking on the phone. Want some new ideas for fun things to do? Here are a few to try:

- Learn a new sport or musical instrument together.
- Create a secret language or code and use it to communicate.
- Volunteer on a project that helps your community.
- Plan a party. Make a video or take photos of the event.
- Make a scrapbook or collage of friendship photos. Or create a friendship journal that you take turns writing in.
- Start a business together. You could wash cars, do lawn work, make crafts to sell, create greeting cards on a computer, take care of people's pets, or find other ways to earn money.

- Start a book club. Choose a book to start with and see that everyone in the club gets a copy from the library or bookstore. Meet to talk about what you've read.

- Join a new club or youth group, such as the Girl Scouts, Boy Scouts, or Boys and Girls Clubs.

CHECK IT OUT!

Boys and Girls Clubs of America
www.bgca.org
This organization focuses on giving young people the skills they need to succeed in life. Many communities have club facilities where kids your age can play sports or games, or just get together to talk.

Boy Scouts of America
www.scouting.org
This program for boys focuses on fitness and character building. Activities include camping, adventure, service learning, and much more.

Girl Scouts of the U.S.A.
www.girlscouts.org
This organization is committed to helping girls develop confidence, determination, and respect for themselves and others. Activities range from sports, science, and service to career exploration and travel—in places throughout the U.S., and in other countries.

If you and your friends are into computers, you probably already know there are fun ways to communicate with each other online. Chat rooms are "live" sites set aside by online services. You and your friends can send electronic messages that appear with other people's messages. The "conversations" in chat rooms can be difficult to follow at first, since so many different people are "talking." You have to be patient as you wait for someone else's response.

A private chat room is one you can set up with friends who are using the same online service as you. If you know your friends' screen names, you can invite them into your chat room, and they can do the same when they know your screen name. What are the advantages over a telephone conversation? You can chat with several of your friends at the same time (plus, if you catch yourself saying something stupid online, you can quickly delete your words before they're sent—something you can't do after they come out of your mouth).

A word of caution: while online, *never* give out your real name, address, or phone number to anyone you don't know or without a parent's permission. If your online service lists members' profiles, *never* write in information that can identify you, such as a description of how you look or where you go to school. And *never ever* send anyone a photo of yourself or agree to meet someone you've talked to online. Remember that people aren't necessarily who they say they are in a chat room.

Communicating online can be fun, but you'll need to follow some rules to protect yourself. The contract on the next page can help you remember to play it safe online. Review it with your mom or dad, and then sign it together. Post it near your computer as a reminder.

Online Safety Contract

- I won't give others my personal information, such as my full name, address, or telephone number, and my school name or address.

- I won't send a photo of myself (or of my family or friends) to someone I meet online without getting a parent's permission first.

- I won't make hurtful or threatening remarks to people I communicate with online.

- I won't claim to be someone I'm not, either by accessing someone else's screen name and password or pretending to be someone else online.

- I will never give out my password. If someone accidentally discovers my password, I'll immediately change it.

- I won't respond to any messages that are threatening to me, my family, or my friends. If I receive such messages, I'll contact my online service immediately or ask a parent to do so.

- I will only meet with someone I communicate with online if I have parental permission and the meeting is in a public place with my parent with me.

- A parent and I will determine rules for going online, including when and how long I can be online, as well as sites or chat rooms I can visit. These rules will be reviewed regularly.

My Signature _____   Date _____

Parent or Guardian's Signature _____   Date _____

myYearbook
myyearbook.com
Founded by two high school students, myYearbook has over 5 million members. This social network connects teens from around the world, giving them access to quizzes, friends' profiles, games, dating matches, charitable causes, and more.

Being a Good Friend

Are you a good friend? And how can you tell? Ask yourself if you're . . .

■ **Dependable:** Do you call when you say you will? Are you on time when you and your friends make plans? Do you keep secrets a secret? Are you there when your friends need help or advice?

■ **Loyal:** Can your friends rely on you to stick up for them? Do you make them a priority in your life?

■ **Supportive:** Do you cheer your friends on in every effort? Do you listen? Do you point out your friends' positive qualities? Are you kind and helpful?

■ **Considerate:** Do you take into account your friends' feelings? Do you make an effort to understand their points of view?

■ **Respectful:** Do you treat your friends the way you would like to be treated? Do you appreciate your friends' unique qualities?

If you answered yes to all of these questions, CONGRATULATIONS! You're a good friend, and that's an excellent quality. Maybe you answered yes to many but not all of the questions. Are you still a good friend? Sure, but you can become an even *better* one.

Decide where you need to improve. Can you call your friend more often? Make an effort to listen? Compliment your friend more? Consider your friend's feelings? Be more respectful? Make an effort to do one thing (or more) each week to be a better friend.

What if a friend of yours is the one who needs to work on his or her friendship skills? It may not be easy telling your friend how you feel, but talking can help. Here's what to do:

- **Agree on a good time to talk.** Find a private place where you won't have to worry about other people listening in.

- **Be honest and direct.** Don't accuse your friend of anything; just calmly explain how you feel. (Take a look at how to use "I messages" on page 74.)

- **Listen to your friend.** If you want your friend to hear what you have to say, make sure you're doing your part by listening.

When You're Not Getting Along

Friendships have highs and lows. Sometimes you and a friend may be so close that you're almost like family. At other times, the two of you may feel so angry with each other that you wonder why you ever became

friends in the first place. How do you keep your friendship strong when you're not getting along? Try conflict resolution.

Conflict resolution is a method of solving problems between two or more people. When you use conflict resolution, you look for an answer that's fair or agreeable to everyone involved. Many schools have conflict-resolution or peer-mediation programs in which kids help work out problems between other kids. Does your school have a program like this? If it does, find out whether you and your friend can get some help with your disagreement. (You may even decide to become a peer mediator yourself. The skills you learn can be valuable outside of school and as you grow up.)

If your school doesn't have a program like this, you may want to help start one. Following is the basic technique that peer mediators use. The two people who are in disagreement can ask a neutral person to help or try these methods with each other.

1. **Decide what the problem really is.** Sometimes the fight has gotten so big that the people involved can't even remember what the original problem was. Or maybe the fight is hiding the real problem.

   For example:

   Renee is hurt and angry that her friend, Ayesha, has been spending a lot of time with a new girl at school. Renee doesn't want to admit how she really feels, so instead she tells Ayesha not to bother coming over Friday night even though they had plans. When Ayesha asks her why she shouldn't come over, Renee says she just changed her mind. Now Ayesha's hurt and angry, too.

   Figuring out the real problem means both sides have to be very honest about their feelings.

2. **Come up with solutions.** Think of as many as possible and make a long list of ideas.

3. **Choose the solution that both sides agree is best.** What would each person like to see happen? Is there an obvious solution? If not, is there a way to compromise? The goal here is to find a *win/win solution,* meaning something positive happens for both people involved. In contrast, a *lose/lose solution* means the "solution" doesn't work for anyone. There are also *win/lose* or *lose/win solutions,* in which the outcome works for only *one* person.

   For example, consider what solutions might work in the following situation:

   Evan has been taking guitar lessons, and his music teacher suggested that he join the school band. Evan decides to give band a try, but his best friend, Mike, gets mad because Evan now has band practice on Thursdays after school. That was the day Evan always came to Mike's house to hang out. Evan feels guilty but is mad that Mike is acting so selfish.

   Possible solutions might include:

   - Evan quits the band and continues to go to Mike's house: *win/lose*
   - Mike stays home alone on Thursday afternoons, while Evan's at band: *lose/win*
   - Evan and Mike stay angry with each other and end their friendship: *lose/lose*
   - Evan stays in the band, and Mike joins the basketball team, which meets on Thursday afternoons. The boys decide to get together on Wednesdays instead: *win/win*

   Now the goal is to agree to *act on* the solution that works best for both sides.

4. **Apologize.** Each person should apologize—and mean it. Forgive one another and put the conflict to rest.

5. **Use a little humor.** There's nothing like laughter to loosen up a tense
    situation. After a serious conversation, it helps to tell a joke or remind each
    other of a time when you did something really weird or goofy. It's hard to
    stay angry when you're laughing!

Friendship Pitfalls

You can't help feeling jealous sometimes. Your best friend gets A's in all
her classes but barely studies. Another friend seems so sure of himself,
always knowing what to say and getting laughs from the crowd. You, on
the other hand, struggle for B's at school and keep your mouth shut in
social situations because you're sure you'll say something dumb. Ouch!
Feel that bite? That's the green-eyed monster of jealousy attacking you—
and your friendship.

How do you defeat that monster? Accept that it's normal to feel jealous
sometimes. But don't let jealousy eat away at you and make you hard to
be around. Instead, think of the positive things you've accomplished. Did
you make the volleyball team? Get a great comment on your latest assignment? Teach your little sister how to inline skate? Thinking of your pluses
will protect you the next time the green-eyed monster tries to strike.

Remember, too, that if something good happens to your friend, it's a *positive* thing. Feeling happy for your friend is a way to show support. If you can't seem to get over your jealousy, ask yourself what's going on. Does your friend have something you want? If so, is there a way you can get the same thing? Instead of putting energy into feeling envious, set a goal for yourself and take steps to reach it. This way, you're focusing on yourself (instead of your friend) *and* using positive thinking to your advantage.

Sometimes jealousy is low self-esteem in disguise. Maybe you feel that you aren't as smart, good-looking, organized, athletic, outgoing, or confident as your friend. Instead of finding ways you don't measure up, think of what makes you stand out. What's unique about you? What are your positive traits? What makes you fun to be with? Take a look at pages 29–34 for more on feeling good about yourself.

Jealousy isn't the only friendship "monster" to look out for: betrayal is a big one, too. A betrayal is a break in trust, such as lying or saying something negative behind a friend's back. Betrayals cause anger and hurt feelings—and can bust up even the strongest friendships.

What if you've betrayed a friend: is there any way to repair the damage? Start by admitting what you've done and saying you're sorry. Apologizing shows that you care and you want to make up. A good friend will probably forgive you if your apology is sincere. Make a promise never to betray your friend again—and keep that promise.

If a friend has betrayed you, talk about what happened. Let your friend know how you feel. If your friend apologizes, try to put the hurt behind you. Any friendship worth having is usually worth saving, too.

This doesn't mean every friendship is meant to last forever, though. People change, and so do relationships. Sometimes friends grow apart and can't find a way to reconnect. At other times, conflicts between friends aren't resolved and the friendship ends. If you've ever lost a friend, you know it can hurt. One way to help yourself feel better is to stay involved in activities at home and at school.

At some point, you may be the one who has to end a friendship. A friend may be doing things that make you uncomfortable—like taking drugs or shoplifting. Or a friend may be too demanding and expect you not to have any other friends. Ending a friendship is hard. You don't want to hurt the person, so what can you do?

Before ending it, decide whether fixing the friendship is possible. Have you talked to your friend about what's bothering you? Sometimes an honest conversation can save a friendship. On the other hand, maybe you've already tried talking things over and you know there's no hope for the friendship. If this is the case, you can try two different ways of ending it:

#1 Be honest and tell the person you want to stop being friends.
This option may be more difficult, but it's the recommended one. When you're honest, the other person knows where you stand. He or she isn't left hanging on to a friendship that no longer exists.

Here are some examples of what you might say:

- "I know we've been friends for a long time, but I don't feel as close to you anymore. Do you feel the same way?"
- "We were close last year, but this year I have new activities, and you have different interests and new friends. Maybe we don't have time for each other right now."
- "I feel like you're into things that aren't right for me, so I can't hang around with you anymore."

#2 You can end the friendship gradually by getting involved in activities that your friend isn't into. This option may seem easier, but it doesn't make it as clear to the other person that you don't want to be friends. In fact, it may take longer for the friendship to dissolve. But some people feel more comfortable letting a friendship fade instead of ending it all at once. Choose the option that's right for you.

TOUGH STUFF

Being the new kid, cliques, bullies, peer pressure. What do they have in common? They're a fact of middle-school life. These situations are tough—but not impossible—to deal with. The best way to handle them is by acting in an assertive way.

For example, what if you come home from school one day and find out the move your parents have been considering is actually going to happen? Suddenly you'll be going to a new home and school—and that means you'll be the new kid. Even if you're looking forward to the move, you'll need courage to make new friends.

Most likely, you won't find a welcoming committee knocking on your door. But some of the kids at school will probably make an effort to get to know you. If some kids seem friendly, see if you can sit with them at lunch, and ask one of them to show you around school or introduce you to other people. Find out if there are other new kids—they'll probably be happy to meet another person who's new, too. Be sure to join some school activities where you'll find people—and potential friends—who share your interests and talents.

If you're unsure of how to approach people, practice introducing yourself and getting a conversation going. You don't have to have an entire comedy routine ready—just think about ways to say, "Hi, I'm _____ (your name)." Rehearse at home, so you get used to saying the words.

When you talk to new people, ask questions and really listen to their answers. Most people are attracted to a good listener. (Besides, you'll have plenty of opportunities to talk about yourself later in the friendship.)

Once you're more comfortable in your new school, you may want to think about starting a "welcome club" to help other new students fit in. Ask your teacher or principal if you can create an information packet, and include a map, a school directory, and fun facts about the school and its teachers. Club members can host tours of the school and invite new kids to join them for lunch. This is a fun way to get to know new people, while learning more about your school.

After you have a new group of friends, you'll feel more comfortable. You'll have people to sit with at lunch, talk to between classes, and spend time with after school and on weekends. All of this will help you feel more at home.

Coping with Cliques

When you're changing in so many ways, belonging to a group can help you feel protected. But sometimes, a group of friends may become too close for comfort. The group may turn into a clique.

Cliques are sets of friends who close themselves off to others. Some cliques leave other kids out or make them feel inferior. These kinds of cliques think of themselves as "better" or more "special." In fact, some of the clique members may convince other kids that the clique is very desirable, just because it won't let them in.

Not all kids in cliques realize how they treat others. In fact, they may not even be aware that they're leaving other kids out or making them feel unwelcome. This is one reason why cliques are so confusing.

A *group of buddies* or a *clique*—you may find it hard to tell the two apart. The main difference is that cliques are usually negative, while groups of friends are positive. Here are some hints for understanding the differences:

Buddies: include people
Cliques: exclude people

Buddies: are loyal to each other
Cliques: have only each other

Buddies: like each other and people outside the group
Cliques: look down on others

Buddies: encourage individuality
Cliques: want each member to be the same

Buddies: enjoy doing things together and apart
Cliques: are hardly ever seen without each other

What happens if you're part of a clique? Ask yourself if that's where you want to be. Often, membership in a clique can make you feel accepted and safe . . . at first. But after a while, you may realize that certain people in the clique act like they're in control. You may have to follow rules about how to dress, talk, and act.

How important is it for you to belong to this clique? Are you doing things you don't feel right about just to make the other clique members think you're cool? If the people you once thought of as friends are now making you miserable, it may be time to break out of the clique. You can find other friends at school or in your community. For tips on making new friends, see pages 96–97.

You don't have to trade your independence for clique dependence. It's up to you to decide which friendships are right for you—and which ones you're better off without.

Cliques, Phonies, & Other Baloney by Trevor Romain (Minneapolis: Free Spirit Publishing Inc., 1998). Everyone wants to have friends, but some kids go too far and join a group that does more harm than good. This book uses humor to show the ups and downs of popularity and cliques. Find out why you don't have to let a bad clique spoil a perfectly good day.

The Ins and Outs of Middle School

Every school has friendship groups. The kids who hang out together often share the same interests—sports, music, academics, and so on. Even in elementary school, you probably knew which groups were considered more popular. But in elementary school, popularity probably wasn't as important.

In middle school, however, groups of kids often start to get labeled. Most kids know which groups are "in," or "out," or somewhere in-between. Unfortunately, the labels become a way to define who people are and where they weigh in on the popularity scale.

Many kids don't care which group they're in, as long as they have good friends to hang around with. They know that labels don't mean much. But some kids will do almost *anything* to be accepted by the "in" group or clique. They copy the group's clothing and language in an effort to be accepted. But often, the harder these kids try to fit in and achieve popularity, the more desperate they seem to others.

Have you ever tried to change your image to fit in with a group or become more popular? If you have, you're not alone. Lots of kids look forward to each new school year as a chance to finally get in with the "popular" group.

The *real* secret to popularity is being yourself. You may have heard that before—that's because it's the truth. Instead of changing your image, work on getting comfortable with yourself. Do the sports or activities you like—not whichever ones are considered "cool." Wear clothes that you feel good in and are comfortable wearing—not ones that match the styles of a certain group. Don't assume you have to be the class clown or downplay your smarts to be accepted. Act confident, even if you don't always feel very confident.

> "Popularity isn't really important. It's an extra—something you can live without."
>
> **DONNA, 13**

Most of all, be aware that popularity isn't a measure of your worth as a person. If you like who you are, it will show. People who feel good about themselves make other people feel good about themselves—and that makes them fun to be around!

Bully Busting

Bullies—every school and neighborhood has them. You probably know who the bullies are in your school; they can be male or female, smart or not-so-smart, popular or unpopular. Hurting or picking on other people gives bullies a feeling of power.

Some bullies like to play mind games. They'll talk behind your back, get other people to make fun of you, and even cause your friends to ignore you—and you may not have any idea why you're the target. Bullies don't need a reason or an excuse to make someone a victim. Sometimes they do what they do because they've learned these behaviors from a parent or another adult. Research shows that many bullies have been mistreated in some way. They bully others to feel stronger and more in control—or because they don't know any other way to act.

If a bully picks on you, you may find it hard to get him or her to stop. Here are some things you can do:

1. **Get your friends to support you.** It's harder for a bully to pick on someone who's surrounded by friends.
2. **Avoid the bully.** Don't be alone in the school hallways, bathrooms, or other places where the bully might find you.
3. **Walk or run away from the bully.** Get to a safe place as quickly as possible.
4. **Talk to an adult.** Go to a parent, a teacher, a school official, your bus driver, or your principal and ask for help.
5. **Tell the bully firmly and assertively to stop bothering you.** You can say, "I don't like the way you're treating me. I'll report you if you keep this up."

You have to know lots of ways to deal with a bully because no *one* way is necessarily the *best* way. For example, avoiding the bully may be impossible if you ride on the same bus. And telling your teacher may not be enough, especially if the teacher doesn't consider bullying to be a serious problem. In some cases, a bully may stop the behavior for a while, only to start up again. You may need to try new ways to get the bully off your back. Don't give up! No one has a right to pick on you, tease you, threaten you, or cause you any other kind of harm.

If *you're* the one doing the bullying, it's time to make a change. Hurting people isn't a way to make yourself feel better. Think about why you're acting this way and where you learned your bullying behavior. Talk to an adult you can trust to give you the help you need.

At some schools, bullies get away with their behavior for way too long. The situation worsens, with the bully becoming more violent and the victim thinking there's no way out. Even if other kids are aware of what's going on, they may be afraid to speak up.

Bullies wouldn't find it as easy to be bullies if people didn't give in to their behavior. Have you witnessed bullying at your school or somewhere else? If you see a bullying incident, get adult help as quickly as possible. Don't try to interfere because you could get hurt yourself.

If bullying is a problem at your school, you can help put a stop to it. Talk to your friends about times when they may have been bullied and ask them how they handled the situation. Find out what they learned and what advice they'd give to other kids who have a bully problem. Talk to your teachers about ways to put an end to bullying. Do your part to make your school a place where bullies aren't welcome.

Bullies Are a Pain in the Brain by Trevor Romain (Minneapolis: Free Spirit Publishing Inc., 1997). If you're sick of being picked on, pushed around, threatened, or teased, this book is for you. Find out what makes bullies tick, and learn how to bully-proof yourself. If you're the one doing the bullying, this book can help you understand why you act the way you do.

Violence in School

These days, news about violence in schools is everywhere. You've probably heard the stories of kids who brought weapons to school and hurt or killed other kids or teachers. You may have experienced violence in your own school. Sometimes bullying is at the root of the violence.

In many cases, kids who feel rejected, lonely, or on the outside blame the rest of the school for their feelings. They get angry and have no way to let the anger out safely. So they reach for a gun and hurt innocent people and themselves. In some cases, a student who acts out in violence is popular, and no one can explain his or her actions. Always, though, kids at school later remember signs that their classmate was having problems.

If you hear someone talking about blowing up the school or shooting people, don't assume it won't happen or treat the words as a joke. Tell an adult right away if you overhear somebody making any sort of threat against other kids, teachers, or school officials. If you know that another student at school has a gun or another weapon, tell a school official *immediately*—even if the person you're reporting is a friend. In many cases of school violence, students later admitted they'd heard kids making threats but hadn't taken them seriously.

School should be a safe place—not a place you're afraid to go. You can help make your school more secure. Here are some ideas:

- Start by getting together a group of kids who are committed to the idea of making your school a safer place.
- Invite a teacher or school official to work with you.
- Publicize your efforts through posters or other outlets such as the school newspaper, radio station, or Web site.
- Help plan a school assembly or program on school safety.
- Ask a teacher to help you involve community groups, such as law enforcement officials, the PTA, or youth organizations.
- Start a peer-mediation program or get involved in the one at your school (for more about this, see pages 103–104).

Handling Peer Pressure

When friends or the kids at school try to convince you to do something you really don't want to do, you're feeling peer pressure. Most kids experience peer pressure at some point during the middle-school years.

You may be pressured about some not-so-serious things—like the clothes you wear or the club you join at school. But sometimes, you may feel pressured about very serious activities—like drinking alcohol, using other drugs, smoking cigarettes, writing graffiti, or shoplifting. What should you do if other people push you to take negative risks? Sometimes, you may be tempted to do what the other kids want you to do just so they'll leave you alone.

Before acting, take a deep breath and try to see the situation clearly. Are all of your friends pressuring you, or just one or a few? If only one or two are trying to make you do something you don't want to do, get your other friends to take your side and reverse the pressure. You may feel more secure making a stand if you've got other people behind you.

On the other hand, you may have to face up to the pressure alone. Standing up for yourself takes courage. That old cliché "Just say no" is way too simple for some of the peer-pressure situations you might find yourself in someday. You may feel that saying no to the crowd will mean losing face or losing friends.

Before deciding what to do, consider what's at stake. What might the consequences of your actions be? Are you taking a chance with your health, safety, or future? If you're worried about what the other kids will think of you if you say no, ask yourself how much their opinion really matters to you. What will taking the risk do to your opinion of yourself? Think through your options before making a choice.

How do you say no and mean it? How do you ensure that people will listen to you and respect your decision? Practice being assertive, so you can say no with conviction. "Um, well, I don't think so, okay?" doesn't sound like you mean it. When you're alone, rehearse what you'll say and how you'll say it. Here are some tips:

1. **Show a sense of humor.** Make a joke or say something funny. For example, if a friend pressures you to smoke, reply, "Yeah sure, a cigarette sounds good, but a cigar would be even better. Ha, Ha, Ha!"

2. **Use a firm no.** You don't have to shout it—just say it assertively. Try "No thanks" or "No, I'm not into that." The more you practice, the easier it will be to respond politely but firmly.

3. **Have a ready excuse.** Some to try are, "That would hurt my sports performance" or "I'm really late—gotta run!" (Then remove yourself from the situation.)

Some people confuse assertiveness and aggressiveness. If you're assertive, you stick up for yourself. You respect yourself and your decisions, and you give honest opinions to your friends. But you don't put other people down. You don't bully others into thinking like you or doing things your way. Those actions are what an aggressive person does. Being aggressive makes other people feel uncomfortable around you. Being assertive earns you their respect.

If you're not used to being assertive, set aside the next couple of weeks to practice your assertiveness skills. Rehearse in front of the mirror, or ask a family member to role-play with you (the family member would pretend to pressure you, so you could practice saying no). Keep at it until sticking up for yourself comes more naturally.

CRUSHES, FLIRTING, DATING, AND MORE

Sometime soon, if not already, you'll probably discover you're interested in certain people on more than just a friendship level. Feelings of attraction are a normal part of growing up. As your body changes, your emotions do, too. In fact, during the next couple of years, you may find that you're very emotional—up one minute, down the next—and some of these feelings are tied to romance.

Often, the first romantic feeling you have is a crush. Crushes are intense, but usually don't last long. You can have a crush on someone your own age, but lots of kids also have crushes on someone older— maybe an older teen, a neighbor, a teacher, or even someone they don't know at all, like a celebrity or an athlete. You can get a crush on someone of the opposite sex, or someone who's the same sex as you. No matter who the crush is on, the emotions are very strong. Yet, crushes aren't true relationships because they're so one-sided. Often, the person you have a crush on isn't even aware of how you feel. Crushes are practice, in a way, for real love.

What's real love? It's a feeling that's hard to describe and understand because it shows itself in many ways. The love you have for your mom or dad, for example, isn't the same type you might feel for a close friend.

And that kind of affection is altogether different from how you might feel toward a boy or girl you're interested in. In fact, you may like someone in a romantic way, but this doesn't necessarily mean you're in love.

To confuse matters, you probably see lots of romantic scenes on TV and in movies. You may think you should have a love life that resembles what you see on the big or small screen. But, the truth is, real life and real teen relationships are hardly ever so passion-filled.

If you're definitely interested in someone, how do you let that person know? One way is to flirt. Some kids are naturals at flirting—most need practice. What does it mean to flirt? You look at the person, smile, give compliments, laugh at his or her jokes. Flirting also includes being genuinely interested in what the person is saying, listening carefully, and giving him or her your undivided attention.

Have you noticed that some people seem to flirt with just about everybody? Some kids flirt to get attention or be noticed. But sometimes, this behavior sends the wrong signals. Being a flirt might make someone think you're interested when you really aren't. Once you know the power of flirting, use it with care.

Do you know the difference between innocent flirting and unwanted attention? Getting noticed by a boy or girl can be flattering. But sometimes, this type of attention isn't appreciated and can take a dangerous turn toward harassment. When a person bothers you in a sexual kind of way, it's called sexual harassment. Here are some examples:

- A boy snaps a girl's bra strap and makes rude comments about her body.
- A girl whistles at a boy every time he passes her in the hallway.
- Whenever two boys sit behind a girl on the bus, they loudly tell jokes or stories about sex.
- Two girls constantly make comments about the physical characteristics of the boys in their classes.
- At the lunch table, a boy regularly makes announcements about changes in the breast size of his female classmates.
- In the gym locker room, one boy constantly tries to snap another boy with a towel.

It isn't always easy for kids—or adults—to recognize sexual harassment and realize how serious it can be. Some people think their comments or behavior are all in fun or are a kind of flirting. They may even think they're giving the victim a compliment. If you're getting attention that makes you feel uncomfortable or unsafe, you could be experiencing sexual harassment. Don't assume the harasser is only trying to be funny or flirtatious.

No one should ever have to put up with harassment—at school or anywhere else. If someone harasses you, you can say something like, "Stop making those comments" or "I don't like to hear that type of thing." However, in some cases, you may not be able to put a stop to the harassment on your own. You can get help from an adult (a parent, school counselor, teacher, or school official). You deserve better than to be harassed.

Dating Dilemmas

What happens if you like somebody, you flirt a little, and the other person responds positively to the attention? Now what do you do?

At some middle schools, kids talk about "going with" or "going out with" someone, "coupling up" or "dating." These terms usually mean a boy and girl are in some kind of relationship. They may sit together at lunch, send emails or notes, talk on the phone, spend time together after school, dance together at school events, or hang out with each other on the weekends—or they may never go out anywhere alone. These relationships may last a day, a week, or a month (sometimes longer).

During the middle-school years, you may feel ready to be in a boy-girl relationship—or not. There's no "right" age to start getting interested in romance. Have you talked about these issues with your mom or dad? Some parents don't allow their kids to date until they're fifteen or older. Depending on your cultural background, your parents may be very strict about this kind of thing. They may not want you to go to dances, parties, or other social events that involve both girls and boys.

If you're allowed to date and you want to explore relationships with the opposite sex, the easiest way to start is in a group. On group dates, boys and girls hang out together, and there isn't as much pressure to be a couple. The advantage of group settings is you get to know members of the opposite sex a little better. And you may even decide that these boy-girl friendships are more important to you than dating right now.

If you've already started dating, be careful about going out with someone older. Being with someone older may seem exciting, but you may feel pressured to get physical in ways you're not ready for. Most kids aren't emotionally ready to get serious about another person during the middle-school years. Even if you and the boy or girl you're seeing are the same age, you may have different expectations about how far to go. The fact is, if someone truly cares about you, that person shouldn't try to make you do things you don't want to do.

At this stage of your life, you probably have a lot of questions about sex. Your mom or dad may have already talked to you about it, and maybe you've learned about the topic at school. You might have looked at books or Web sites to get more information. Most likely, some of your friends and classmates are confused about sex, too. Sometimes, kids try to seem sophisticated and knowledgeable about sex, when they actually aren't. You may hear "facts" that aren't true, which can confuse you more.

Instead of relying on friends and other people your own age for information about sex, go to an adult you trust. Talking to a parent or other adult about touchy subjects may feel uncomfortable at first—for both of you! But once you get over the initial embarrassment, discussing sex becomes easier. Being open about the subject can help you now and as you face more decisions in the years ahead.

What if you don't feel ready for all this boy-girl stuff and you're not interested in dating right now? You may be afraid other kids will think you're uncool or immature if you don't want a boyfriend or girlfriend, but it's totally normal to wait a while before getting involved in romantic relationships. Lots of young people don't become interested in dating until their high school years or later. There's no rush. Do what feels right to *you*—not your friends or other people you know. If your friends are intense about dating and are pressuring you, explain to them how you feel. If they continue to push you, you may need to look around for friends who share your values and beliefs.

Real Friends vs. the Other Kind by Annie Fox, M.Ed. (Minneapolis: Free Spirit Publishing Inc., 2009). Learn insider information on making friends, resolving disputes, and dealing with other common middle school concerns like gossip, exclusion, and cyberbullying. Get expert advice on crushes, peer pressure, and being a good friend.

Sex, Etc.—A Web Site for Teens by Teens
www.sxetc.org
Produced by the Network for Family Life Education, a component of Rutgers University School of Social Work, this site is dedicated to preventing unwanted pregnancies and sexually transmitted diseases in teens. The site includes frank articles on a wide variety of topics related to sexuality, sexual health, and sex education. Visitors can send in their own questions or read other people's Q & A's.

Your First Kiss

When you were younger, the idea of a romantic kiss probably seemed sort of gross. But lately, it may not seem that way at all. In fact, now that you've entered the middle-school years, you may be very curious about kissing—and hoping your first kiss will happen soon.

During the next few years, you may find yourself in more kissing situations. For example, you may be invited to parties where the entertainment includes kissing games like Spin the Bottle. Participating in these kinds of activities isn't *required.* If you don't feel ready to kiss someone in a game like this, you can say so. If the people you're with are true friends and they respect your point of view, they'll understand.

On the other hand, maybe you're eagerly looking forward to the chance to kiss someone you like. You probably see a lot of kissing on TV and in movies. In fact, by now you've probably seen hundreds of on-screen "smooches" that take place in romantic settings with swelling music. Is real-life kissing like that? Sometimes. But the perfect kissing you see on TV and in movies is completely scripted and planned out. The actors—who've been carefully made up, dressed, lighted, and filmed by professionals—have rehearsed every move.

Lots of kids your age wonder what kissing feels like or how to kiss the "right" way. Some kids practice their kissing techniques on mirrors or on their arms or hands, and you can try that if you want to. But the best preparation of all is knowing you're ready to kiss or be kissed.

Kissing can happen almost anywhere and at any time. Maybe you're just talking to your boyfriend or girlfriend, or you're getting ready to say good-bye after having spent a fun day together—suddenly there might be a pause, and the moment seems right. You may ask, "Can I kiss you?" or move toward the other person gently, which is a way to ask without words whether it's okay. If the other person seems willing, go ahead and kiss. (Otherwise, STOP.) When you're kissing, try not to judge the experience too much. Lots of first kisses involve colliding foreheads or noses.

A note about kissing and telling: it's natural to want to tell your friends about your kissing experiences, but remember, the person you kissed may not want the details spread all over school. Some things are best kept to yourself.

███

During the next few years, you'll probably face all sorts of new "firsts"—your first school dance, crush, or kiss, for example. These firsts can be exciting. Others may be very hard-to-handle—like your first experience with intense peer pressure or a clique, or your first big fight with a friend. You won't always know how things will turn out, but you can do your best to be prepared.

Talk to some adults or older siblings about what to expect and how to handle new situations you might face. Even more important, ask yourself what's right for you when it comes to friendship, peer pressure, dating, and other aspects of the middle-school social scene. Do you know what's important to you? Do you know how to take care of yourself? To stick up for yourself or stand up for what you believe? Remember to stay true to you!

MAKE THE MOST
of SchooL

School—you spend at least one quarter of every weekday in the building, and when you add up your homework time, your club or sports time, your time getting ready in the morning and "de-stressing" after school . . . wow, school gobbles up a large chunk of your life! School should be more than just a place to see your friends every day (although that's not a bad start)—and definitely more than something you have to "get through." This is where survival tip #6 comes in: making homework bearable, doing well on tests, working on projects, participating in activities, and discovering how to enjoy learning. Here are lots of ideas to help you succeed in school.

SURVIVING MIDDLE SchooL

Is middle school different from elementary school? In a word—YES! You may have had different teachers for special classes like art or gym in elementary school, but now you've probably got a different teacher for every subject. The upside is that each teacher is a specialist in a particular area: Your science teacher will have lots of training in science, just as your social studies teacher will have special knowledge of history and government. Is there a downside? Perhaps that it's a little harder to get to know your teachers—and help them get to know you—when you see them for less than an hour each day.

Another difference is that many middle schools have homerooms. This will be your home base at school and the first place you go each morning. Homerooms serve as important sources of information (attendance, announcements, sign-ups) for you. Your homeroom teacher will most likely teach you in at least one other class.

Along with a homeroom, you may also be assigned to a locker. This is your place to store all the notebooks, folders, and textbooks you're not using at the moment. If your locker doesn't already come with a combination lock, you can buy one. Memorize the combination and practice using the lock before putting everything you own in your locker. If you have two lockers, one for books and one for gym clothes, you may want to buy a pair of locks with the same combination (they're sold as a set).

Another change from your elementary days is the amount of classwork, homework, projects, and tests you'll have. Now that you're older, you can handle more assignments. But you'll have to plan your time much more carefully, especially if you tend to feel stressed out when you have a lot to do. (You'll find tips on time management on pages 166–168.)

> "In elementary school, boys and girls are told to stand in separate lines, and then they're walked to the library or wherever. In middle school, you're told, 'Now everybody, just get to the library.' There's no teacher or hall monitor following you."
>
> **MATT, 13**

The biggest difference in middle school, most kids say, is that you're expected to find your own way. You're not led around by an adult who makes sure you're handling your assignments properly or getting to your next class on time. This doesn't mean you're *entirely* on your own. Your school probably has administrators, guidance counselors, and other adults who will offer help when you ask for it. The key here is you have to *ask* for it.

What about your very first day of middle school? Feeling nervous is normal. Being prepared helps, so try the following tips:

- Talk to kids who've already gone through at least one year at your middle school to find out the most important things you'll need to know.
- Find out where the bathrooms are before you need to get to one in a hurry.
- Bring some extra money for phone calls, just in case you need to contact your parents. (Be sure to carry their work phone numbers along with you, as well as the names and numbers of other people you can call in an emergency.)
- Remember to bring a lunch or money to buy one at the cafeteria. (Having your mom or dad show up with your forgotten lunch isn't the best way to make a good first impression.)
- Bring pencils or pens and at least one notebook for jotting down home-work assignments or supplies you'll need.
- Check with the bus driver right away to make sure you've gotten on the correct bus.

Many elementary schools schedule an orientation in the spring or summer—long before the first day of middle school. That's the time to find out critical pieces of information, like the location of the nurse's office, bathrooms, and public phones. Take notes during orientation and keep any handouts you've been given, since you may forget important details over the summer.

If all else fails, remember this important tip from fourteen-year-old Rob, who survived middle school and even his first few days of high school: "Don't panic because you think no one can help you. If you ask enough people, someone is sure to have the answer or assistance you need."

Getting Along with Your Teachers

Teachers are people, and people have a wide range of personalities, attitudes, and likes and dislikes. You'll get along better with some than others, just as you do with your classmates. Most teachers want you to succeed—they don't believe it's their job to torture you (even though that thought might cross your mind when it's almost midnight, and you still can't answer one of your homework problems). Think of it this way: the more successful you are in school, the more successful your teachers feel. Try to think of you and your teachers as partners in learning.

Once in a while, you may come across a teacher you have trouble getting along with. What can you do? Try to figure out what the teacher regards as important. Most teachers make their priorities clear at the beginning of the school year. If a certain teacher expects class participation, make an extra effort to get involved in class discussions. If another teacher believes neatness is crucial, work hard at handing in papers that don't look messy. If getting your work finished on time is important to one of your teachers, do your best to meet deadlines. Just remember that every teacher is an individual—get to know each of them and help them to get to know you.

Sometimes in the process of getting to know a teacher—especially one who's really terrific, young, or attractive—you may develop a crush. This happens to lots of kids and is usually temporary. Daydreaming about your teacher is normal (even typical) at your age, but acting on this type of romantic fantasy is *never* okay. If you're confused about your feelings for your teacher or uncomfortable with something he or she has said or done to you, talk to an adult you trust.

> "Your teachers expect much more from you now than they did in elementary school. But most of them are willing to help if you're willing to approach them."
>
> **SAMANTHA, 13**

What about teachers you don't like? Or just can't seem to get along with no matter how hard you try? If you're unlucky enough to have a teacher who yells a lot or is highly critical of students, there *is* one consolation. At least you're in middle school, which means you don't have to spend all day with that teacher! If the situation is unbearable, ask a parent or school administrator to get involved. But before that, give your teacher a fair chance by talking directly to him or her first.

What are your teachers like? Just for fun, rate them:

Your teacher is so smart you could check an encyclopedia's accuracy against his facts.

Or:

Your teacher is still trying to find out where the faculty bathroom is.

Your teacher explains the subject so well that you could hold a conversation with a classmate and still understand the lesson.

Or:

Your teacher's explanations are so fuzzy that even *she* can't understand them.

   While few teachers are as exaggerated as these, you'll soon learn that some teachers are definitely better than others. Some are so inspiring you'll remember them for the rest of your life. Others won't be quite so memorable. And then there are those teachers you'd soon like to forget!

What makes a teacher great? Many kids say their best teachers are those who:

- recognize that every kid is an individual with different needs, interests, and strengths
- are intelligent and realize that students are smart, too
- show enthusiasm for the subject and for teaching it
- understand that there's often more than one way to solve a problem
- are creative in the assignments they give
- assign homework to help a student learn (not just to give more work)
- make learning fun

"My favorite teacher was like a kid in many ways. She wore overalls, stood on the desk, and gave out fake money that we could trade in for things like a pencil sharpener or a book. She would also do impersonations of things and people. She was fun, but at the same time, she made you work hard."

CHARLOTTE, 11

When you have a special teacher, do your part to nourish that relationship. A teacher can be your mentor, helping you discover what you love to do and encouraging you to pursue your talents. A teacher can also be your friend—someone to go to when you have a problem at school or in your personal life. And a great teacher can even inspire you to be great yourself!

Using Your Brain

Have you noticed that you know a lot more than you used to? Facts, statistics, dates, formulas—thousands of pieces of information are stuffed somewhere in your brain ready for action when needed. Where did they all come from? Reading, listening to music, tasting new foods, looking up at the night sky, even watching TV. Sure, some of that information isn't exactly *useful* (like knowing the jingle to the latest fast-food commercial). But you're probably finding that digging through that growing warehouse of information in your brain allows you to figure out the answers on tests or to do your homework problems. Not only do you have more information available to help you answer questions, but you're also developing more complex ways of thinking and solving problems.

Maybe you've also found that, once in a while, you just can't retrieve a specific piece of information at the precise moment you need it. How many times has it happened to you: you're taking a test, and you can almost *see* the fact on the page, but it just doesn't come into clear enough focus? After the test, you rush to the textbook and, of course, there it is, clear as day—the formula you needed. The good news: you'll probably remember that fact for a long time. The bad news: five points have been deducted from your test score.

Learning something well is a way to retain information, instead of just memorizing facts for a test. Learning involves constant reviewing. You may have to read something again and again before it sinks in. You may also have to write it down to remember it. And after that, you may still need to review the information several times before you finally get it. (Check out the "Study SMART" tips on page 134.)

What's one other change you may have noticed in your thinking? You can do it a lot faster now. Your younger siblings or cousins probably don't catch on to stuff as quickly as you do. You may be pleasantly surprised at how much you know and how fast you can solve problems compared to when you were in elementary school. Try to be patient with younger kids, who might not get things as quickly as you do.

Even when kids are the same age, they have different abilities in their thinking, problem solving, and level of knowledge. That means you can teach your friends, and they can teach you. Not a bad deal!

Putting Your Creativity to Work

One of the smartest ways to use your brain is to put your creativity to work. Do you think that being creative means painting an extraordinary sunset or composing fabulous music? Those are good examples, but you can express your creativity in less amazing ways and in other ways than through the arts. In fact, you can use your creativity to become a better student. How? By coming up with an original idea for a health-fair project, developing several solutions to a problem in science lab, or figuring out a unique way to better your community.

If you think being creative is a quality you have to be born with, think again. Every kid can learn to become more creative. Whether you already see yourself as creative or you view yourself as one of the least imaginative kids on the planet, you can unleash your creativity with some practice. All you have to do is learn to think in new directions and let your ideas pour out. Get comfortable with brainstorming, or writing down any thoughts that come to your head. Pick and choose the ones that are the most interesting and see where these thoughts lead you.

To be a more creative person, take a little time each day to do something imaginative and fun. Here are some ideas:

- Try a craft or hobby like woodworking, making collages, or working with clay.
- Start a collection and think of a unique way to display it.
- Paint, draw, or sketch. Or design a Web site, picture, or newsletter on the computer.
- If you sing or play a musical instrument, make up a song.
- Take photos and display them in interesting new ways.
- Create something using a needle and thread, paper, ink, flowers, music, cloth, words, glue, wood, or any other materials that interest you. Get new ideas from magazines, art books, hobby shops, or nature.

Studying Smart

While some kids seem to just breeze through their homework and barely need to open a book before a test, most have to study to do well. Here are some ways to make the most of your study time:

- **Get organized.** How can you study if the place where you do your home-work is a mess? Spending time looking for a pencil or a dictionary can be a waste. If you have your own room, clean up your desk and keep it neat and organized. If you share a room, keep a box or crate with your homework supplies handy and tote them to a quiet spot.

- **Make sure you have the tools you need.** Did you bring your textbooks and assignments home? (Teachers hate it when students use the old excuse that they couldn't do their homework because they forgot to bring home their books!) Do you need a calculator for your math problems? Will you have to do research at the library or online? Do you have access to a computer or an encyclopedia? If you don't have all the tools you need, can you get a ride to the library or borrow materials from a friend?

- **Pick a quiet spot with few distractions.** Make a rule that when you study, you won't turn on the TV or take any phone calls. If you don't want to miss your favorite television show, videotape it to watch later. Music is a "maybe"—some people can study with music on, while others find it distracting. Figure out what works best for you.

- **Make sure you have a good reading light and a comfortable chair.** It's not helpful to struggle to see in dim light or strain your shoulders or back while sitting in a chair that's too hard, too soft, or the wrong size for your desk or table.

- **Keep a study calendar.** Use a calendar or daily planner to record your assignment due dates and to write down the times and days you plan to study. Each time you make a study date with yourself, do your best to stick to it.

- **Have a positive attitude.** Homework isn't a punishment—even though it might feel that way sometimes. Think of homework as a way to train your brain and prepare yourself for upcoming tests.

Here's a way to study SMART:

Skim the chapter headings, the notes at the back of the chapters, and any charts and graphs.

Make a note of the main points and important details of each chapter as you read.

Ask yourself questions as you go along to see if you understand the material.

Review your notes and underline the important information.

Take a break every thirty or forty minutes. Then see what you can remember before you start studying SMART again.

Taking Tests

It's 10 P.M., and you have a science test tomorrow. Do you break out in a sweat just thinking about it? Or did you start worrying as soon as your teacher announced it? Is your heart pounding now just reading about tests? Or are you one of the lucky few who stays calm?

Tests are a regular part of middle-school life. You probably have more tests now than you did in elementary school—sometimes you may have more than one in a week. That's why test anxiety can become a regular part of the middle-school experience for many students.

Getting somewhat anxious about tests is normal. It may help to know that a little fear can actually be a *good* thing. The stress you feel can motivate you to study and try to do your best. If you're too relaxed about an upcoming test, you might not bother studying at all, and this could lower your score.

Some kids in middle school get so anxious that they can barely concentrate before or during a test. This type of fear isn't productive—in fact, it can make success nearly impossible. If you're extremely anxious about test-taking, here are some things you can do to prevent the fear from making you forget even your own name:

- **Study.** This is an obvious tip, but it's also the most helpful one. The more you know about a subject, the more comfortable you'll feel going into the test. Overprepare if you think it might help.

- **Talk to your parents.** They've been in lots of test situations themselves and may have some helpful hints you can try. (If they don't, you've at least given them an opportunity to go down memory lane, something most parents love to do.) Ask them to quiz you or help you better understand the material.

- **Talk to your teacher.** Let your teacher know about your fears and ask if he or she can offer tips for calming down. You can also ask for suggestions about what to study.

- **Learn some easy relaxation exercises you can do before and even during a test.** Try this one: Close your eyes, imagine a pleasant scene— riding an ocean wave or laughing with friends, for example—and take a couple of deep breaths. Then open your eyes and go back to your test. (See page 61 for some other stress-reducers you can use to decrease your overall anxiety level.)

- **Tell yourself you can do well.** (Just try to do this quietly during the test.) If you say things like, "I know the formula for energy" instead of, "I know I'm going to fail this test," you'll feel more confident. In fact, you just might be amazed at the difference positive thinking can make!

- **Create and take practice tests at home.** This helps you get into your teacher's head. What is she likely to ask? Try answering those questions. What is she *not* likely to ask? Try answering those questions as well (especially if you're not a talented mind-reader). Some teachers may even provide a practice test, if you ask for one.

- **Form a study group with some friends.** Each member can spend some time acting as the teacher (that means teaching, not doing impersonations!). One of the best ways to learn a subject is to explain it to others. Discuss the material and quiz each other. To make sure you actually study instead of fool around, set some ground rules for each study-group meeting. Take breaks every so often to keep yourselves interested and alert.

▦ **Tell yourself it's just one test.** (There will be lots more!) If you mess up or don't do as well as you'd like, remind yourself that it's just one test—not the end of the world.

Successful athletes say that the ability to forget about a misstep is one of the keys to doing well. A basketball player who misses an easy shot can't keep focusing on his error if he wants to play well during the rest of the game. When a figure skater falls in the middle of a routine, she doesn't just lie there on the ice (unless, of course, she's broken her leg). She gets up, continues to skate, and thinks about what's next instead of what went wrong. In both cases, the athletes put the mistake behind them and focus on the rest of their performance. You can do the same in test situations.

Successful School Projects

Yikes! Mr. Fischer has decided his class needs a challenge—you've been assigned a PROJECT! Never fear. A project is just the "extra large, extra cheese, extra pepperoni pie" of homework. Slice it up, and you can finish it in no time—with no indigestion! Here's how:

1. Are you doing this project with a team? If you're working with a group, try to decide what your piece of the project will be as soon as possible.

2. Find a way to make the project interesting for you. For example, if the environment is important to you, your science project could focus on that. Think you'd like to be a doctor someday? Try a project about the human body. Adore animals? Into sports? A music lover? A techno-whiz? Let your project mirror your hobbies and interests, so it's more fun for you to do.

3. Once you know your part of the project (or if you're working alone), break the entire assignment into smaller tasks and set a deadline for completing each one. For example, you may need to do some research, so your first

goal could be to go to the library on Wednesday after school. By Saturday, organize the information you've collected and see what other research you may need to do.

4. If you're working with a group, make a schedule. Meet regularly at a place with few or no distractions—the mall would *not* be a good place to work, of course.

5. Make the project look good. If it's a research paper, make sure it's neat and think about using a folder, a binder, or a cover page. Consider fun, unusual, or artistic ways to present your information.

6. Set a date to finish the project at least one week before it's due. An early deadline allows you time to look over your work and make any necessary changes.

7. Giving a presentation? Practice in front of an audience (your family or some close friends who promise not to make you laugh).

8. Making a video? Be sure your equipment is working and available. You don't want to find out at the last minute that the camera battery is dead.

9. Doing an experiment? Make sure it works and that all your supplies are ready to go.

10. Finished! Reward yourself for a job well done, and then look forward to the next time you can show off your project skills.

Working on a project with a partner or within a group is typical at most middle schools. Pairing up this way can be a good tool, because as you and your partner share knowledge, you *gain* knowledge. Teaching others reinforces your own understanding of a subject.

Most teachers try to be fair about how kids are paired, making sure that everyone has a partner, and that different kids get a chance to work with each other. But not every partnership turns out to be a successful one. You may feel that you've been assigned to a partner or group that will be difficult to work with. Before judging, give the other person or people a chance. You may change your mind about the situation once you get to know each other better.

Here are some more tips on pairing up for school projects:

- If the teacher assigns partners and you've been overlooked, speak up. Your teacher has a lot of kids to manage and may not notice if you've been left out by mistake. If he's not aware that you don't have a partner, he can't help you.

- If you're allowed to choose partners, look for someone who can complement your strengths. Suppose you know a student who's a good writer and you've got artistic skills—just imagine the possibilities if the two of you were to hook up!

- Once you have a partner, spend time learning more about each other's interests and talents. What can you each add to this joint project? Maybe you're great at building things or you know how to organize a report well—don't be shy about mentioning what you're good at.

- Do your share as a partner, but don't overdo (or *under*do) it. Pull your weight, even volunteering for some of the less-appealing parts of the project. But don't take over, even if you believe your talents will help your team earn an A. Part of the reason for working with others is learning to cooperate and complete something *together.*

Whether you're working on a project with a group or alone, start by doing some brainstorming. You can use the worksheet on the next page to come up with ideas for topics, research, and more.

...... Project Ideas Worksheet ......

Topic ideas: _____

_____

Title ideas: _____

_____

Supplies and books needed: _____

_____

Research to be done: _____

_____

People to interview: _____

_____

Steps to take:	Dates for completion:
1)	
2)	
3)	
4)	
5)	
6)	
7)	

Presentation ideas: _____

_____

Project due date: _____

Preparing Reports

You may have done a few reports in elementary school, but in middle school, reports are a BIGGER deal. They're longer, for starters. And you may be expected to use more resources for your research. In addition, middle-school teachers expect you to use even more creativity when putting together reports. Are you up to the task? Sure you are!

Reports, like school projects, are hard work and they demand a lot of time. As with school projects, breaking down the assignment into steps can help. Start with a brainstorming session and figure out what topics you'd like to explore. Make a long list, writing down any ideas that pop into your head, no matter how off-the-wall they may seem. Read over the ideas and choose the ones that appeal to you most. Now ask yourself these questions: *Can I find enough information on this topic? Will too many other kids in the class be tackling this topic, too?* Try to pick an idea that's not only original but will also be possible to research. If your teacher has already assigned the topic, brainstorm new and different ways to present it.

You can do research using books, encyclopedias, magazines, and CD-ROMs, or by searching the Internet. A CD-ROM is packed with information—a complete encyclopedia (the volumes that take up two shelves on your bookcase) can fit on a single disc. And the amount of information on the Internet is growing all the time. You can find educational publishers, encyclopedias, museums, and university libraries online.

Whether you're doing your research electronically or with print publications, follow these basics:

1. Don't try to read every word of a Web site, article, or chapter you've found. Instead, skim to see if you've located the exact information you need, and then make notes. Keep printouts or photocopies of the materials, if possible, so you can refer to them later if needed.

2. Don't plagiarize, which means copying word-for-word the information you've found and putting it into your report. By law, you can only copy the words if you're quoting the material and using footnotes. If your teacher suspects that something in your report is plagiarized, she can check to find

your original source. Learn from other people's ideas, but then express those ideas in your own words.

3. Analyze your research to decide if it's useful or helpful. Ask questions like: *Is this a reliable source? Is the information current? Is it accurate? Is it complete?*

After you've finished researching, you're ready to make an outline to follow. What information do you want to cover? Which ideas should be presented first? What comes next? After that? What conclusions can you draw? An outline can guide you through the writing process.

Next, you can begin to write. At this point, you don't need to worry about spelling, grammar, or making "perfect" sentences. Just get your ideas down in a first draft. When you're done with that draft, read it carefully so you can make revisions. And remember that *no one*—not even famous authors—writes a perfect first draft. If you're using a computer, you can easily move sentences and paragraphs around. It's a good idea, however, to keep printouts of your old drafts, or save them on a disk, in case you want to go back and look at material you might have changed.

Are you happy with what you've written? Did you express yourself clearly? Did you follow your outline? Is there any information you left out that should be added? Anything you want to delete? Make any final changes, and then begin to check your grammar and spelling.

Many computer programs have spellchecks that will help you spot errors. Even so, don't depend on your computer to catch every misspelled word. Review your report carefully because your computer will read a word like *he* as spelled correctly, when you really meant to type *the*. You can also have your computer check your grammar, but as with the spellcheck, it's not always the best "teacher." Be sure to review your work carefully yourself, and even ask a family member to look it over for mistakes, too.

Your family and friends can also help you determine if your report is complete and interesting. Ask somebody you trust to read the report and offer comments. Try not to get discouraged by any criticism you might receive. Instead, look at it as feedback that can help you make your work even better.

Allow time to do a final rewrite. You may think of ways to make your writing clearer, or you may want to add a fact you forgot. When you're happy with the rewrite, decide how you're going to "format" your report (how you want it to *look*). Most reports are printed in a twelve-point font or type. Check that your margins are even and include page numbers if you need them. You can add a "header" or "footer" that will print your name, the title of your report, and the page number on every sheet. The better you get at formatting, the more interesting you can make your reports look!

If you know how to use a desktop publishing program, you can make your report resemble a newspaper, a magazine, or a journal. Graphics and tables also add interest to school reports. Depending on the computer and software you're using, you may even be able to turn your report into a slide show, video, or animated movie. If you have a special digital camera, you can take photos that load directly into your computer's memory. Programs for drawing, painting, or designing on screen allow you to make adjustments to your photos and text. Add some music, and you can create a multimedia extravaganza that will surely dazzle your teacher and classmates!

A word of warning: *Always* be sure to save your work onto a disk or in a file in the computer's memory before you print a copy. (To be extra cautious, save to the hard drive *and* to a disk.) You can even set the computer

to automatically save your work every five minutes or so. This will prevent you from experiencing a major school-report disaster—like losing everything you've written!

Learning Styles, Learning Difficulties

You, like everybody else, have your own unique style of learning. Do you prefer to have a newspaper article read to you, so you can imagine the event as it's being described, or do you prefer quietly reading to yourself? Does music help you study, or does it distract you? Have you found that you learn better when you have an opportunity to *do* something, rather than just hear a lecture? Use what you know about yourself to find the most effective way to study and do homework. And remember that the learning style that works for your friend won't necessarily work for you.

In addition to having a preferred way to learn, you know you're more capable in some areas than in others. In a middle-school classroom of twenty-five kids, a few may have special abilities in math or music, while others may show superior athletic skills. Some may be gifted in the way they understand and deal with people, while some may have a knack for writing and communicating. Some kids are strong in many areas, while others are exceptionally talented in one particular skill.

Take a moment to think about your own strengths. What do you get excited to learn about? What do you love to do? Is there a certain class you shine in? Are most classes easy or hard for you? Is school enough of a challenge? Are you feeling bored in some classes?

If you feel that you want more of a challenge, here are some suggestions:

- Get involved in an after-school activity—perhaps a theater group, the school newspaper, or the chess club. This can help you feel more creative and interested in what your school has to offer.
- Think of ways to make your assignments more exciting. Instead of writing a paper about how the heart works, for example, you could design a Web site on the topic or create a battery-powered model.

- Ask your guidance counselor about opportunities for advanced study open to middle-school students. Local high schools, colleges, or universities, for example, may offer summer programs. You might also be able to get involved in a long-distance program in math, writing, a foreign language, or another subject.

- Find out if your school has a program for gifted and talented students. Talk to your teacher about whether you may be qualified.

For some kids, school is a real struggle. If you're having a tough time, you know how discouraging it is to put a lot of effort into your work and still do poorly. You may need to learn different strategies for taking notes or studying. A guidance counselor or a teacher may be able to help. If your school has a tutoring program, try that out. Ask your mom or dad for help in a subject that's giving you trouble. You may need to try a few of these options before you notice an improvement in your grades.

If your learning problems continue, you may have a learning difficulty. What does this mean? It doesn't mean you're stupid or that you can't learn. You're as smart as other kids your age, but perhaps you're not processing information, perceiving words in a book, or recognizing numbers on a page the way other students do. If this is the case, you may need to get special help at school. Ask a teacher, parent, or school counselor how you can get the help you need and are entitled to receive.

The Gifted Kids' Survival Guide: A Teen Handbook by Judy Galbraith, M.A., and Jim Delisle, Ph.D. (Minneapolis: Free Spirit Publishing Inc., 1996). Written with the help of hundreds of gifted teenagers, this book is the ultimate guide to understanding high ability, accepting it as an asset, and making the most of who you are.

The Survival Guide for Kids with ADD or ADHD by John F. Taylor (Minneapolis: Free Spirit Publishing Inc., 2006). This book explains ADD and ADHD and offers strategies for how to take care of yourself, modify your behavior, get along at home, enjoy school, have fun, make friends, and deal with doctors, counselors, and medication.

The Survival Guide for Kids with LD (Learning Differences) by Gary Fisher, Ph.D., and Rhoda Cummings, Ed.D. (Minneapolis: Free Spirit Publishing Inc., 2002). Kids who are having trouble learning still can learn—they just do it differently than other kids. Find out what learning differences are, how to tell if you have one, why LD makes it hard to learn, what LD programs are, and how to succeed throughout the school years and beyond.

What Can Your Parents Do to Help?

Do you rarely ask your parents to help you with homework or projects? Or do you think you can't get your work done without a parent helping you? Maybe you rely on your mom or dad for help in certain subjects but not others?

"Adults should have to go to school for a day to see what it's really like for us. Things have changed so much—what we learn, what the kids are like, and just about everything else."

KEVIN, 12

Many parents enjoy this role and can help with getting homework done or preparing for tests. Just be careful that you're not relying on your mom or dad *too* much. It's still your homework and your test—not theirs. That said, your parents can do a lot to help support you as a student. They might:

- help create a well-lighted, quiet, private work space for you at home
- suggest books and Web sites you can look at for homework help or information for a report or project
- brainstorm ideas with you when you're trying to figure out a topic or a strategy for a report or project
- look at an outline you've prepared before you start the actual writing of a report or paper

- review your paper, project, or report after you've finished a first draft and suggest minor changes (don't have them rewrite—that will improve only *their* writing skills)
- ask you questions to help you review for a quiz or test
- review a test you've already taken to help you understand why certain answers were marked wrong
- celebrate a great report card with you (not with gifts or money, but with congratulations on a job well done)
- encourage you to work harder when you receive a grade that's below your potential
- listen to you when you gripe about a teacher, test, or classmate, and then offer advice for handling the situation
- suggest ways you might talk to a teacher in a class you're having trouble with, or one in which a classmate is bothering you
- help you brainstorm ways to make school more challenging
- act as an advocate for you when you're in a difficult situation at school (meaning they might talk to your teacher, a guidance counselor, or even the principal)
- read this list, so they'll know what *you* now know about how they can best help you in school!

SPORTS, CLUBS, AND OTHER ACTIVITIES

School isn't just about tests, reports, and homework. Most schools provide kids with lots of opportunities for extracurricular activities—before or after school, and on weekends or holidays.

Athletics are a major part of the school experience for a lot of kids. In fact, for some kids, joining a team is the most natural thing in the world. Maybe they've been playing soccer or softball since their elementary-school days. However, some kids don't want to go near a ball—even if their lives depended on it. (Well, maybe that's an exaggeration! But it's true that some kids dislike sports or don't consider themselves to be athletic.) How would you describe *your* feelings about sports?

If you happen to have talent for a sport or a strong desire to play, you can look into joining a community travel team. These teams choose players through a competitive tryout system. Travel teams play against other teams in an area—sometimes a very large area. Travel teams often take trips to other cities, or even other states, for games or tournaments.

If you're interested in a sport but don't want to make the kind of commitment a travel team requires (like getting up at dawn on a cold Saturday to prepare for a game), this type of team probably wouldn't be right for you. On the other hand, if the idea of competition and hard work excites you, consider trying out. If you're new to a town and are interested in participating in tryouts for a travel team, talk to your gym teacher or call the local parks and recreation department.

Many communities and schools organize intramural teams, which are less competitive than travel teams (at least in the way kids qualify). Most intramural teams are set up to allow people of all abilities to play. So if you've been wanting to try basketball but haven't had a lot of playing time, you could join an intramural team. See if your gym teacher has information for you, or ask some other kids at school or in your neighborhood. Some kids join both intramural and travel teams. Because kids are often placed randomly, be prepared to play against your close friends.

School teams generally fall somewhere between travel and intramural teams. You may have to try out, but school teams often don't require the kind of time commitment that travel teams do. One advantage of playing on a school team is that you get to be known, and sometimes even admired, by other kids—which has its benefits in middle school.

To find out what kind of team experience might be best for you (and your family), take the following quiz.

TEAM QUIZ

DIRECTIONS: On a separate sheet of paper, write whether you: strongly disagree, disagree, agree, or strongly agree with each statement.

1. I don't mind getting up very early on a weekend if I can play on a good team.
2. Receiving harsh criticism really bothers me.
3. My family is willing and able to take me to games and practices, even at night and on weekends.
4. Sports are important to me but not one of my top three interests.
5. My friends say I'm a great athlete.
6. I'm not a very competitive person.
7. I'm good at managing my time.
8. I'm in pretty good physical shape, and I'm prepared to work hard to stay that way.

9. I wouldn't want to have to devote myself to one sport more than another.

10. Focusing on academics is way more important to me than being a top athlete.

What do your answers mean?

If you agreed with statements 1, 3, 5, 7, and 8, you're a good candidate for a travel team. If you strongly agreed with at least three of them, travel teams are probably ideal for you.

If you agreed with statements 2, 4, 6, 9, and 10, you might enjoy an intramural team. And if you strongly agreed with those items, intramural team, here you come!

How to Start Your own Club or League

You may find you're interested in an unusual sport that your school or your community doesn't offer—sumo wrestling? curling? badminton? (All Olympic sports, by the way.) Or maybe you want to start a community intramural team, so you can play your sport but not have to try out. Or perhaps you enjoy sports of the mind, like chess, debating, or interactive card games—and you want some other kids to play with. Maybe you're more interested in forming a hobby club based on an activity like photography or collecting. How do you get started—and get others involved?

1. **Make sure your community or school doesn't have the club or sport you want.** (Maybe you just missed the announcement in the park and recreation league's newsletter. Or perhaps the club at school is small, and you just haven't heard about it.) Try your religious organization, the Police Athletic League, a health club, or youth groups like the Boys and Girls Clubs or Girl Scouts or Boy Scouts to see what might be available nearby. Come up empty? Go to step 2.

2. **Find out who else might be interested.** If you're trying to organize a team, you'll need enough players. Sometimes you can start out with just a

few kids because others will join once the news spreads. If you want your club or sport to be recognized by your school or community parks department, you'll need a lot of members to join at the same time. (Your school and community administrators require reassurance that you'll actually use the time and facilities set aside for you.) To advertise, talk to your friends, put up flyers or posters, get in touch with a reporter at your school or community newspaper, and ask for an announcement to be made at school. If other kids express interest, write down their names and save them as proof that you have enough potential members. Suppose you've done so and a bunch of kids want to join—now what?

3. **Get someone to sponsor you.** If you want your sport or club to practice or meet at school, you'll have to talk to the administration. Most likely, you'll need a teacher to act as the club's sponsor or coach. Pick a teacher who's likely to say yes and show him or her the names of all the kids who are ready to join. Maybe the teacher will even talk to the administration on your behalf. If not, you can go directly to the administration office and state your case. (Practice what you're going to say beforehand. You'll want to be especially convincing about the need for your club or sport.) If you'd like your group to be part of the community parks program, you'll need to talk to the person who runs that department. It may help to get some parents involved, especially ones who are willing to act as club sponsors or coaches.

4. **Find out about a national organization that may exist for your hobby or sport.** You can find the contact information on the Internet or in a magazine about your club or sport. The national organization may have resources to help you start and run a local group.

5. **Set some ground rules.** Choose a time and day to meet, and decide on any rules you'll need to follow. Make sure everyone gets a copy of this information. As a group, figure out whether dues are necessary, and then elect or appoint someone as treasurer. You'll probably need to have a club leader or team captain, too (maybe that's you).

Once your club or league is up and running, have fun and feel proud. What an accomplishment!

PREPARING FOR THE YEARS AND CAREERS AHEAD

You already know that the study habits you develop now will prepare you for your life as a high school or college student. And if you're not too pleased with those habits (or the grades you've been getting), you might want to go back to some of the information earlier in this chapter for a brief refresher course.

It's not too early to start thinking about high school and higher education. The courses you take now are the foundation for the subjects you'll study in high school. And some kids will even have an opportunity to take high school-level courses while they're still in middle school.

Make an appointment with your school guidance counselor or advisor to find out about special opportunities. (For example, if you receive very high scores on standardized tests, you'll be able to take a more advanced standardized exam while you're in seventh or eighth grade and be eligible for special programs during the summer and by mail or computer during the school year.) If you want to go to college, be sure to start taking the kinds of classes that will best prepare you for the high school courses that are important for college.

In addition to thinking about the school years ahead, you may start wondering about career possibilities. You may already have a good idea about what kind of work you'd like to do—or not. Either way, you've got lots of time before you actually have to decide. And once you're working, it's likely that you'll make a couple of job shifts as your interests, needs, or circumstances change.

Is there a job you're dreaming about, but you wonder if it's too far out of your reach? Maybe you love to sing or dance, but those careers seem so competitive that you're wondering if you should become an accountant instead. Or maybe you want to be a poet, but people are already telling you that you'll need to get a "real job" first. Perhaps you want to own your own company, come up with an amazing invention, or help solve the world's hunger problem. Don't ever give up on a dream—even one that doesn't seem to have a high probability of success. If you want something badly enough, you can work to make it happen!

Maybe you have no idea what you want to do with your future. Or perhaps you have so many interests that it's hard to imagine one particular path. What can you do now to explore various career options? Here are some ideas:

- Take advantage of a school holiday to go to work for a day with a parent or another adult family member.
- Read biographies or autobiographies of successful people in a variety of careers.

- Join school clubs or get involved in extracurricular activities (such as making costumes or building sets for the school play) to get some experience in areas you haven't yet investigated.
- Practice skills that will be important in *any* job—time management, assertiveness, conflict resolution, problem solving, and decision making. It's never too early to get a handle on these skills.
- See if your school has career videos to check out.
- Remind yourself of how much time you'll spend at work during your lifetime—and how important it is to pursue a career that will be fun and challenging. People who work because they love what they do are always the most satisfied in their careers.

As a middle-school student, you're developing habits, skills, and ideas that will set the stage for your success in high school, college, and beyond. You can see school as a place you hate to go (and an experience you have to get through), or you can view it as a place that can help you develop your mind, your body, your talents, and your interests. Do you look at school in a different way now than you did when you were younger? Growing up means you're beginning to recognize that you can turn opportunities into accomplishments—and feel proud of the kind of student you're becoming.

TAKE CHARGE
of YOUR LIFE

Change. That's what the middle-school years are all about—changes in your body, your appearance, your feelings, your family relationships, your friendships, your school day. So much change can make you dizzy. At times, you may feel that you're losing control. What can you do to get yourself back on track—to rediscover the real you underneath all these changes? You can try taking charge of your life. That's what survival tip #7 can help you do.

DECISIONS, DECISIONS

The older you get, the more decisions you need to make and the more difficult the decisions become. When you were younger, your family made many decisions for you—even picking out the clothes you wore and the activities you participated in. But as you get older, you take on more of the decision making. You become more independent. And with your growing independence come some difficult choices.

You make decisions every day. Some are easy—what you're going to eat for breakfast, for example. Some may be harder—two friends have separately invited you to do something Friday night. And some decisions may

TAKE CHARGE OF YOUR LIFE   155

. . . .

be *very* hard to make—like you don't want to visit your dad and stepmom during school break.

Every decision involves a choice. You have to choose what to do or what to say (or sometimes you may choose to do or say nothing). Making the best choice can be difficult. But you can follow a set of decision-making steps to help the process go more smoothly.

#1 Decide what the real issues are. Suppose you don't want to visit your dad and stepmom during your school break. Ask yourself the reason why—and be honest about it. Do you not want to go because you and your friends have made exciting plans? Or is it because you still feel upset about your parents' divorce and your father's remarriage?

Knowing what the true problem is can help you make the best decision. If your reason for not going is because you're angry with your dad, then not going may be a bad decision: you'll hurt him, and ultimately yourself, because the two of you won't have a chance to work on your relationship. If your reason for not going is because you have a heavy schedule of sports and other activities with friends, then not going may be a good decision: you need to fulfill your responsibilities to your team-mates, and you may be able to visit your dad during the next school break instead.

How do you figure out what the real issue is? You can:

- talk about your dilemma with family members and friends
- write about your problem in your journal
- set aside some quiet time to reflect on your choices
- discuss your feelings with a sympathetic and trusted adult—a school counselor, youth group leader, or teacher, for example

#2 Review your options. Make a list of the choices you have before you. If two friends want to get together with you on the same night, you could:

- go out with one friend and tell the other no
- stay home
- suggest the three of you do something as a group

If your decision is a difficult one, consider the pros and cons of each option. Write them down, think about them carefully, or discuss them with a neutral person. Here are some examples.

- **Going out with one friend:** the *pro* is that you'd make one friend happy, but the *con* is that your other friend may have hurt feelings.
- **Staying home:** the *pro* is you don't have to say no to anyone, but the *cons* are that you might not have much fun alone and your friends may be disappointed.
- **Doing something as a group:** the *pro* is you *all* get to have a good time—maybe there's no *con!*

#3 Make your decision. Set a reasonable deadline for yourself—anywhere from an hour to a week, depending on the difficulty of the decision. Then pick one of the actions from your list and follow it.

Sometimes, even when you make the best decision you can, you may not get the results you wanted. This can be a learning opportunity.

Suppose you have to decide between continuing piano lessons or taking voice lessons instead. You talk to your family and your music teacher to get their opinions. You write in your journal about what to do. You list the pros and cons, set a deadline, and make a decision to stick with piano. But after a few weeks, you start to wonder if you've made the wrong choice.

Now what? Do you agonize over it or get mad at yourself for picking the wrong thing? No, because you can always make a new decision. Life is full of interesting choices—and each one you make will lead you in a new direction. Sometimes you need to just enjoy the adventure and discover where your decisions will take you!

TAKING CARE OF NUMBER ONE

Making decisions that are the right ones for you can be very difficult if your friends or classmates are making some not-so-good choices themselves. Suppose you want to eat healthy foods, but your friends are "snack-a-holics," consuming junk food at lunch and for snacks. Do you do the same, so you don't stick out? What if your friends are taking illegal drugs, smoking cigarettes, or drinking beer or other types of alcohol? You know these activities are risky, but you don't want to be left out or teased. What do you do?

Sometimes, you may forget to take care of yourself because you're feeling stressed out or pressured by friends. Even if you know you should eat right or avoid unhealthy activities, you may tell yourself it's easier to just go along with what your friends and other people your age are doing. At other times, you may be talked into stuff because you're tired of disagreeing. And at still other times, you may simply be curious about trying something you haven't tried before—especially if your friends are talking about how "cool" it is.

Take smoking as an example. What if your friends are doing it, and you start to think they're cooler or more grown-up than you are? Maybe you see lots of advertisements that show smokers looking healthy and sophisticated, and you want to look the same way. Perhaps you've seen your favorite movie star smoking, and you think having a cigarette may make you more like the person you admire. Should you give in? No way!

Before kids who smoke took their first puff, they all had the chance to make a decision—a healthy one or an unhealthy one. Give yourself time to check out all

"A boy in my class is always talking about smoking, like it's a really big deal. But I think he's just trying to get attention."

JULIE, 11

the facts. Contrary to what you may have heard, smoking doesn't help you lose weight, feel more energetic, reduce stress, or relax you. Like other drugs, nicotine is addictive and you'll be a lot healthier without it.

Almost all people who started smoking when they were in middle school wish they hadn't gotten into the habit—just ask them.

CHECK IT OUT!

Most schools offer information about the dangers of smoking, drinking, or taking illegal drugs. Have you talked to a parent about these issues? Having a conversation about these activities can be really difficult for parents. Although they want to protect you and keep you healthy and strong, they may not know what to say or how to say it. Even though talking about these issues can be uncomfortable, it's important to know your family's feelings and values. And talking only to your friends can give you lots of *mis*information. To find out more, check out the following resources:

1-800-662-HELP, or 1-800-662-4357, connects you to the Center for Substance Abuse Treatment (CSAT) of the Substance Abuse and Mental Health Services Administration. When you dial this number, you'll hear a recording that leads to more options, such as alcohol and drug information, treatment options in your state, and counseling. You'll need to use a Touch-Tone phone.

1-800-729-6686 is an information line for the National Clearinghouse for Alcohol and Drug Information (NCADI). This federal organization provides free information on drug and alcohol abuse. You can call 24 hours a day, seven days a week. Online, go to: *www.ncadi.samhsa.gov/links*.

1-800-788-2800 will connect you to all federal alcohol and drug clearinghouses for free information about alcohol and drug abuse. You'll get a recording that will provide options for reaching other information and help lines. Call from a Touch-Tone phone.

Al-Anon and Alateen
www.al-anon.alateen.org
This site includes information on Al-Anon, a worldwide organization designed to support families and friends of alcoholics, and Alateen (for younger members). You can find out more about the organization, decide if you want to join a group, and locate meetings in your area.

Foundation for a Smokefree America
www.anti-smoking.org
This site offers background research on the effects of smoking, tips for people who want to quit, and examples from a marketing campaign designed to expose the damage smoking can cause to the body. You'll also find links to other anti-smoking Web sites.

Taking care of yourself—putting yourself first—means doing what's best for your body and for your emotions, such as:

- eating right and exercising
- avoiding unhealthy habits (like cigarettes, alcohol, and drugs)

- making positive decisions
- being with friends who respect your values and positive choices
- making an effort to manage your time and your schoolwork
- keeping a good relationship with your family
- holding on to your self-esteem

Doing things you don't want to do or giving in to negative peer pressure or media messages means you're putting yourself *last.* Learn how to stick up for yourself and be assertive. Peer pressure is very intense during the middle-school years and being "different" can be hard. But taking care of number one may mean saying no to the bad decisions your friends and peers are making. The truth is, most kids really admire people who are able to stand up for themselves and make decisions that show self-respect.

> "If you have the 'right' friends, they aren't going to pressure you to do the wrong things—like drugs."
>
> **JESSE, 14**

If you're having a hard time making healthy decisions, talk to family members, teachers, or other trusted adults. Getting the advice of people who care about you can help you make smarter choices. Plus, people who are older than you have made lots of different decisions in their lives (probably some of the same ones you're facing) and their experiences—both good and bad—are worth learning from.

If your friends continue to pressure you to do things you don't want to do or if they're a bad influence in your life, you've got some decisions to make. What are your options? You might:

- dump your friends
- go along with your friends, so you won't have to argue
- try to get your friends to stop doing what they're doing
- stick up for your beliefs and values

Each of these choices has pros and cons, but the final choice, sticking up for yourself, is the very best one. Can you see why?

Taking Risks

Good risks vs. bad risks: How do you tell the difference?

Bad risks are dangerous—they can hurt your body or your mind. For example, attempting a dangerous skateboarding stunt without a helmet or knee pads is a bad risk. So is drinking alcohol when you're underage, or taking illegal drugs anytime.

Good risks, on the other hand, help you stretch yourself. If you take a challenge such as performing in front of an audience or participating in a new activity at school, that's a good risk. Positive risks mean trying something you're not 100 percent sure you'll do well—but going for it anyway because you believe in yourself enough to take a chance.

Some kids enjoy physical risks—they're "thrill seekers," and they like the adrenaline rush of extreme sports or other physical feats. Other kids shy away from these kinds of activities but love challenges such as entering a contest, participating in theater, doing a service project, giving a presentation, or running for a class office. All of these experiences, whether they challenge your body or mind (or both), can be positive risks.

If you're a natural risk taker, it may be easy for you to meet new people or try out the latest roller coaster. Your challenge may be to curb your impulse toward dangerous risk taking—like trying things you're not prepared for physically or mentally.

If you tend to avoid risks of almost any kind, however, you may need to find ways to break out of your comfort zone and explore new opportunities. For example, suppose you love to sing. You sing in the shower, you sing in your room along with your favorite groups—but you would never dare do it in public. What if you forget the words? What if you sing off-key? What if . . . ? The "What ifs" can stop you from taking the good risks that help you grow and add excitement to your life.

At some point during middle school, you may have a chance to run for student government, take the lead on a class project, try out for a sports team, or start your own business—all positive risks. But if you focus on negative what ifs, you might not take the risk at all. Instead of imagining the *worst* that can happen, consider the *best* that can happen. Focus on the positive what ifs: *What if I succeed? What if I feel really good about myself for taking a chance? What if I build my confidence and self-esteem?* That's the way to pump yourself up to try something new.

Not taking the risk to do something you want to do is a lot worse than taking the risk and failing. After all, you can always try again! You can figure out what went wrong and take steps to fix it. And now that you've had at least one "practice run," you'll have a better idea of what (and what not) to do next time.

Want to know the best part about pushing yourself to take a risk? You'll learn a lot about yourself and what you're capable of doing. You'll also earn respect from your friends and family for giving something your best shot.

MANAGING YOUR MONEY AND YOUR TIME

Managing your money and your time are two more important ways you can take charge of your life. During the middle-school years, you have new opportunities to make money—and more choices for how to spend what you earn. You also have more options for how you spend your time—and more activities, schoolwork, family responsibilities, and friends to juggle. Managing your time and money wisely is a tricky balancing act—but one you can handle if you learn to make good choices.

Money Matters

Do you already earn your own money or get an allowance from your parents? If so, where do you fit on the money spectrum: a spender, a saver, or somewhere in-between? Some people have a hard time handling money; it always seems to disappear from their grasp. Others know how to hold on to what they've got and keep making more. But most people probably fall somewhere in the middle; they spend money on things they really want and try to save a little for the future—but they don't have a clear idea of what their budget is.

Many kids learn their money habits from their families. Families have different approaches to money—and different rules about it, too. Many kids receive an allowance, for example. In some families, the allowance is based on the number of chores kids do. In other families, the allowance is given freely whether or not the kids do work around the home. And in still other families, kids earn a fixed allowance but do extra chores for extra money. Some parents simply don't believe in giving kids an allowance or have any extra money to spare.

If you earn an allowance, chances are you're wishing for more than your mom or dad pays you. Do you feel you deserve to have your allowance raised? Maybe it's time to talk to your parents about your expenses. Do you need more money for school supplies, clothes, or materials for your hobby?

Think about how to approach your parents about this issue. Don't pick a time when they seem grumpy or rushed, or when money is especially tight at home. When the time is right, you could start the conversation by telling them some good reasons for giving you a raise. Have you been doing more chores? Buying more basics for yourself (clothes, shampoo, notebooks)? Saving for a big purchase? Give your parents a chance to share their point of view, too. There may be many reasons why they can't raise your allowance—or pay you anything at all. If this is the case, you need to think about earning some extra cash on your own.

You're still too young for a job in a fast-food place or a store, but that doesn't mean you can't find other work. If your family has its own business, for example, you may be able to earn extra money by pitching in there. Or your family may know people who are willing to pay for chores like raking, mowing lawns, cleaning homes, walking dogs, babysitting, gardening, or shoveling snow.

If you have a skill or talent, you may be able to turn it into cash. Adults who need help with computers are a good source of income, for example. Are you good at creating Web pages? Can you design newsletters or do special graphics? Are you skilled at Internet research? Can you diagnose computer problems accurately?

Are you handy with a screwdriver and other tools? Start a business that helps people put together furniture and other unassembled products. Good at sewing? Offer to hem clothing or repair split seams. Do you have a talent for crafts? Create and sell jewelry, picture frames, scrapbooks, T-shirts, greeting cards, or other items.

As a one-time money-raising event, you could hold a tag sale. Start with the items you no longer want, and then offer to clean out the garage and closets, and with your family's permission, sell the items they no longer want. You can invite friends to bring items to sell and help you on the day of the sale. Other ideas include holding a bake sale or creating a talent show and charging admission, if you know other kids who are interested in participating (of course, you'll have to share the profits). Make sure you post plenty of signs to advertise your special event, and then take them down afterward.

What do you do with the money you earn as an allowance or from a business? Make a budget! A budget helps you keep track of how you spend and save.

When you budget your money, you need to record your *expenses* (the money you spend) and your *savings* (the money you have left after paying your expenses). Expenses can fall into two categories: (1) fixed expenses, which don't change, and (2) flexible expenses, which do change. Fixed expenses might include the amount you need for buying your lunch at school or what you spend on materials for your business. Flexible expenses might include entertainment like movies, magazines, compact discs, or gifts for your friends. You can spend less on your flexible expenses if you want to have more money to save. Use the budget sheet on the next page to track your expenses month by month.

MY BUDGET

	WEEK 1	WEEK 2	WEEK 3	WEEK 4	TOTALS
EARNINGS:					
FIXED EXPENSES:					
FLEXIBLE EXPENSES:					
SAVINGS:					

You can keep your savings in a piggy bank or stuffed in a drawer, but a smarter place would be in a savings account at the bank. You might also save your earnings in a money market account or CD (certificate of deposit), both of which you can learn about at a bank. All of these accounts allow you to earn interest, or an amount the bank gives you for use of the money you've deposited. Banks have different interest rates and programs, so check out a few before you decide where to put your money. Your mom or dad can help you with this process.

Another option is to invest your savings in shares of stock. That means you own a small percentage of a company of your choice. Or you can look into mutual funds, which let you invest small amounts of money in a large number of companies. You can usually make more money by investing in stocks or mutual funds (compared to keeping your money in an account at the bank), but these investments are much riskier—you can lose money if the value of your stocks goes down. Learn more about investing before you decide what to do. You can talk to a family member to get more information, or perhaps find a relative or family friend who has a job related to business or investing. You can also do research online at sites that offer investment information.

Time Matters

You only have twenty-four hours each day to do all the things you want to accomplish, and sleeping is going to take a large chunk of that time. You may be discovering that getting older means having a lot more to do—and evidently less time to do it in! You've got homework, activities, family responsibilities, and friendships to handle. Maybe it seems like the hours zip past, and you still have lots to do. Maybe you feel that you need more time for yourself.

Managing your time well can make your life a whole lot easier. Did you know that managing your time is a skill you can learn?

Often, kids don't realize how much time they spend on stuff that isn't that important. What usually happens is that they run out of time for activities that *are* important or more enjoyable. Take television, for example. The average kid watches about twenty-five to thirty hours per week, and this can be a real time-waster. Other activities that can eat up your time include talking on the phone, playing electronic games, hanging out in chat rooms, and surfing the Internet—if you spend hours doing them.

This doesn't mean you have to spend every waking moment doing something productive! Sometimes you need time to unwind. You can daydream, doodle, hang out in your room, or lie back and watch the clouds drift by. These activities give your brain and body a chance to rest and gather the energy you'll need for more active pursuits.

To find out if you're making the most of your time, keep track of what you do for one week and how much time each activity takes. (Focus mainly on your time before and after school.) Record the time you spend on activities like sports, music, or clubs, as well as time spent with family and friends. Make a note of what you do during your alone time, too.

After one week, review your list of activities. Put a 😄 next to the ones you enjoyed and a 😦 next to the ones you didn't. Put a ✓ next to the activities you *had* to do. Place an ✕ by any nonessential activities you could have left out or shortened. Then draw a ☆ next to the activities you wish you could have spent more time on.

Now study your list. Are there a lot of frowns and Xs? Maybe you can find ways to cut out activities you don't like or cut down on time-wasters.

Maybe you've got a lot of stars on your list? If so, can you find more time to do these activities you enjoy?

Do you have lots of check marks? This could mean you have too many responsibilities right now and not enough time to be with friends or by yourself. Is there an activity you're willing to give up to make time for other things? Ask a friend or an adult to look at your list and give you some suggestions.

One way to make the most of the time you have is to create to-do lists each day or week. These lists help you see everything you need to accomplish. Start by making a list of all your tasks and responsibilities, and then rank them in order of importance. Those are the things you must do first. Will some of your high-priority tasks take a lot of time? Break them down into shorter assignments and put those in order of importance. Cross off each job you complete. If you want, make a new list of the things you still have left to do.

Many kids use calendars or day planners, as well as to-do lists. These tools allow you to see your days, weeks, and months at a glance. You can keep a record of appointments, scheduled events, and other important activities. You'll probably find that writing things down encourages you to better plan your days and stay focused on meaningful activities.

But what if certain tasks just aren't getting done? Maybe you keep shuffling them to new days on your calendar or transferring them from one to-do list to the next—also known as procrastinating. Procrastination is putting off and putting off and putting off what you need to do, until the very last moment. Then you reach a point where you feel totally stressed out because the deadline is approaching and you haven't made any progress. You end up rushing around, feeling frustrated and upset, and not doing a very good job.

A lot of people have a problem with procrastination, including adults. Few people look forward to doing things that aren't much fun or that seem difficult. Waiting until the last minute is a way to get out of the job—until the last minute arrives, the big job isn't done, and time has almost run out. Other people put off doing things because they expect perfection of themselves. They feel so much pressure to be "the best" and to do a "perfect" job that they're overwhelmed before they even get started.

Goal setting is a skill that can help you beat the procrastination blues. The key here is to set *realistic* goals—ones you have a good chance of reaching. You can set a goal to become more physically fit, for example, or to save more money. Or you can aim to make some new friends or to complete a school project on time. Goal setting isn't a difficult skill, but it takes practice. You decide on the steps you'll take to reach each goal and the date you plan to complete each one.

How do you start? Decide on a goal that has meaning to you. Goals can be long-range or short-range. Long-range goals are ones you want to reach in the future—six months or a year from now, for example. Short-range goals are more immediate—ones you hope to achieve in a matter of days or weeks. Start by thinking long-range. What do you *really* want? Higher grades on your report card is a worthy long-range goal, for example, and one that will take time to accomplish.

Now think of some *manageable* short-range goals that can help you reach the big goal. Maybe you'd like to do well on your next math test or turn in your social studies homework on time this week. List the steps you'll need to take to accomplish these short-range goals. When do you need to take each one? Set a target date. To keep track of your progress and any problems you may encounter, use the guide that begins on the next page.

▪▪▪▪ GOAL SETTING GUIDE ▪▪▪▪

MY LONG RANGE GOAL: _____

MY TARGET DATE FOR REACHING IT: _____

THREE SHORT-TERM GOALS TO HELP ME GET THERE:

SHORT-TERM GOAL #1 _____

THE FIRST STEP: _____

MY TARGET DATE FOR TAKING IT: _____

THE SECOND STEP: _____

MY TARGET DATE FOR TAKING IT: _____

THE THIRD STEP: _____

MY TARGET DATE FOR TAKING IT: _____

OTHER STEPS AND TARGET DATES MAY INCLUDE: _____

_____

_____

SHORT-TERM GOAL #2 _____

THE FIRST STEP: _____

MY TARGET DATE FOR TAKING IT: _____

THE SECOND STEP: _____

MY TARGET DATE FOR TAKING IT: _____

THE THIRD STEP: _____

MY TARGET DATE FOR TAKING IT: _____

OTHER STEPS AND TARGET DATES MAY INCLUDE: _____

_____

_____

Continued on next page ⟶

▪▪▪▪ GOAL SETTING GUIDE ▪▪▪▪
(CONTINUED)

SHORT-TERM GOAL #3 _____

THE FIRST STEP: _____

MY TARGET DATE FOR TAKING IT: _____

THE SECOND STEP: _____

MY TARGET DATE FOR TAKING IT: _____

THE THIRD STEP: _____

MY TARGET DATE FOR TAKING IT: _____

OTHER STEPS AND TARGET DATES MAY INCLUDE: _____

_____

_____

IDEAS FOR STAYING ON TRACK WITH MY GOALS: _____

_____

_____

POTENTIAL PROBLEMS: _____

_____

_____

HOW TO DEAL WITH THEM: _____

_____

_____

PEOPLE WHO CAN HELP ME: _____

_____

_____

Goals are something you do for *you*. It's a waste of your time and energy to go for a goal you don't believe in or want for yourself (for instance, a goal that's important to your mom or dad but doesn't hold much meaning for you). When setting your long-range and short-range goals, ask yourself why you value these accomplishments. Are they truly meaningful to you? Will they make you feel good about yourself and the person you're becoming? If so, then go for it!

Making Time for a Hobby

With all you have going on in your life, you need to spend some time doing something FUN. Hanging out with friends is fun, and so is watching movies or reading a good book. But there's something else you can do, too—something relaxing and energizing. What is it? A hobby.

Hobbies are a fun way to excel, take a healthy risk, and try something new. You can share a hobby with a friend or family member, or do one on your own. Kids have all kinds of hobbies—common ones like playing a sport or collecting trading cards, or more unusual ones like beekeeping. If you have a hobby that you love, you already know why hobbies are important. But if you don't have one, you may be thinking, "With school, my family, and my friends, who has time for a hobby?" Actually, a hobby is a great thing to *make* time for. When life seems to be going a mile a minute, a hobby can be a relaxing escape. And when your life is going well, a hobby can add to the pleasure you're already feeling.

Hobbies are active—they help develop your mind or body. And they give you a way to explore life beyond what you learn in school. A hobby you have now can stay with you your whole life, like a familiar friend who's always interesting and there for you. Some hobbies may even become careers.

If you don't have a hobby or you'd like to find a new one, take the following quiz. Your answers may point to interests you didn't know you had.

. . . .

HOBBY QUIZ

DIRECTIONS: Pick either A or B for each question. Write out your choices on a separate sheet of paper.

Would you rather be:

A indoors

B outdoors

Which do you enjoy more:

A winning

B playing the game

Do you prefer to spend your free time:

A alone

B with others

For a vacation, which would you rather do:

A visit a city and go to museums, shows, and the theater

B go hiking and camping in a national forest

Do you prefer to contact your friends by:

A email

B notes on your own handmade paper

When you're bored in class, do you:

A cover your page with doodles

B daydream about being outdoors

Are you more of a:

A pack-rat

B neat-freak

If you're forced to wait in a long line, do you:

A take out the book you brought with you to read

B mentally rehearse scoring a goal

After school, would you prefer to:

A play ball or do some other physical activity

B look at a magazine

If something is broken in your house, do you:

A try fixing it yourself

B read and explain the directions to a family member who's willing to make the repair

Take a look at your results. Did you choose answers that involve being outdoors or doing something physical? Did you pick ones that show you like to do things with your hands? That you enjoy mental challenges? That you're competitive by nature? Did your answers reveal that you like to be involved with other people? Or that you prefer pursuing activities on your own? Did you learn something new about yourself?

Below is a list of different types of hobbies. See if you can find one that matches your interests.

- **Creative expression:** watercolor painting, oil painting, murals, sculpture, drawing, photography, creative writing, bookmaking, jewelry-making, poetry, drama, music, singing, needlepoint, woodworking, journaling
- **Physical activities:** hockey, soccer, baseball, basketball, football, volleyball, hiking, biking, running, dance, cheerleading, gymnastics, horseback riding, inline skating, ice skating, snowboarding, skiing, skateboarding
- **Collecting:** stamps, coins, dolls, rocks, shells, miniatures, trading cards, cars, comics, action or animal figures, key chains, books, model trains or airplanes
- **Nature exploration:** hiking, orienteering, bird watching, gardening, animal care, experimenting, chemistry, sand sculpture
- **Intellectual exploration:** reading, computers, building models, foreign languages, astronomy, crossword puzzles, trivia, chess, historical reenactment, video games, board games
- **Home arts:** pottery or clay, crafts, sewing, knitting, quilting, embroidery, weaving, cooking, scrapbooks, basket making

Note that some hobbies fit in more than one category. Horseback riding, for example, is a way to explore nature or to compete with other riders. Rock collecting can involve outdoor hiking, studying the origin of different specimens, and coming up with a creative way to display your treasures. Hobbies can be as unique and diverse as the people who do them!

Making Time for others

Want to know another valuable way to use your time? Giving it to others. Volunteering your time, energy, and skills helps you feel that you're making a contribution to the world (and you are!). Lots of kids your age have found that volunteering makes them feel good about themselves.

You may already be active in your community, pitching in for a worthy cause. Or maybe you volunteer through your religious organization or youth group. Some schools require students to perform a number of hours of community service—does yours? If you haven't been involved in any type of service project, you may wonder if your busy life is too full to fit in one more activity. Before you decide not to volunteer, consider the benefits of taking the time to do for others.

Being of service can give you a chance to give back—to make the place you live better by cleaning up a park, painting a mural over a graffiti-filled wall, or starting a community vegetable garden in a vacant lot. Volunteering can provide you with an opportunity to connect with other people—senior citizens at a nursing home, adults or kids in a shelter, or new kids who have moved to your community. And volunteering can offer a way to let your voice be heard—writing letters about a cause you believe in or joining an organization that shares your ideas and values.

Kids who volunteer gain new experiences and broader views about life—they expand their vision of the world. When your vision of the world grows, so does your vision of *yourself*. Volunteering means accomplishing—and whenever you accomplish something, you increase your self-esteem.

Look around you. What needs to be done? Who needs to be helped? Where can you give a few hours of your time?

CHECK IT OUT!

The Kid's Guide to Service Projects: Over 500 Service Ideas for Young People Who Want to Make a Difference by Barbara A. Lewis (Minneapolis: Free Spirit Publishing Inc., 2009). Pick a topic that interests you—animals, community development, crime fighting, the environment—and then flip through this book to find ideas for all kinds of service projects you can try.

The Kid's Guide to Social Action: How to Solve the Social Problems You Choose—and Turn Creative Thinking into Positive Action by Barbara A. Lewis (Minneapolis: Free Spirit Publishing Inc., 1998). Get inspired by stories of real kids around the world who are making a difference, and then use the step-by-step social-action guides so you can make a difference, too.

ROLE MODELS AND MENTORS

Growing up is hard to do completely on your own. Having help from role models and mentors who have been through what you're going through can make an enormous difference.

A role model is someone you admire so much that you try to use that person's life as a pattern for your own. Good role models encourage you to aim higher and be the best you can possibly be. A mentor is someone who's available to help and advise you—in a hobby, a potential career, school, volunteer work, or any other aspect of your life. A role model and a mentor can be the same person (but don't have to be).

Do you have a role model? You don't have to know him or her personally. Many kids use sports figures or famous heroes as their role models. Look for someone who has overcome disadvantages or tough times and ended up successful. And remember that success isn't necessarily about being rich, famous, or powerful. Success can mean helping others, being generous, or acting with courage.

If you want to have a role model you can talk to, look for someone you know who has created the kind of life you'd like to lead yourself. Your role model can be a teen or an adult. Maybe the person is a great parent, donates time to the community, or is a talented achiever in a field of work you're interested in. Can you think of anyone right now who might make a good role model for you? If you need ideas, talk to a friend, parent, or teacher.

What happens if a role model you've chosen lets you down? Maybe you always looked up to a certain sports star—someone who gave you the courage to try out for a team and work hard in athletics. Now you've just heard this same star has been arrested for using drugs. How do you feel? Betrayed? Angry? Shocked? You've just learned that someone you thought could do no wrong made a mistake—a serious one. Will that role model continue to be one for you? It depends on what he or she does next.

Your role model might admit the mistake, apologize, and change his or her life for the better. In fact, that person may become even more of a role model, making better decisions in the future and helping others do the same. Or maybe the person continues making poor decisions, each one followed by an excuse or a refusal to admit any guilt. Role models are human, not superhuman, and like the rest of us, they make mistakes. You can still learn from these people, even if you don't look up to them like you did before. And you can take satisfaction in knowing that the person helped you, in some way, to make positive changes in your own life. Then you can look for a new role model to admire.

What about mentors? A mentor is a person older than you who can act as your guide and advisor. Many adults who enter the business world find a mentor who can help them achieve success in their careers. You can look for a mentor to help you navigate the middle-school and high-school years. A mentor might be a member of your family or a neighbor, teacher, coach, Girl Scout or Boy Scout leader, religious advisor, youth group leader, member of your community, or an older brother or sister of a close friend. An organization like Big Brothers/Big Sisters of America may be able to set you up with a mentor as well (check your phone book for a listing for this organization).

Research shows that kids who have mentors find it easier to make healthy decisions and positive choices in their lives. Having at least one adult to confide in—someone who has experienced the challenges of growing up and making decisions—can help you stand up for yourself and stand strong against negative peer pressure. If you know your mentor is in your corner, cheering you on in your efforts, you gain added confidence as you take charge of your life.

WHAT'S NEXT?

Soon you'll be in high school and considering college, a trade school, the military, or a career. While those days may seem far, far in the future, they're actually not. You probably thought middle school was a long way off when you were a little kid—but look how quickly you got here!

Do you ever daydream about your future? What are these dreams like? Do they include an exciting career, a romantic relationship, travels to amazing places, possibly some (terrific) kids and a nice home? Do daydreams have to be realistic? Not at all. Maybe you imagine exploring Pluto or climbing Mount Everest. Whatever your dreams are, they're telling you something about yourself. And they're offering you a safe way to explore careers, lifestyles, and desires for your future. As you try each one on for size, you get a chance to see if it fits—and if it doesn't, you can begin a new dream, one that's more suited to you.

"I just finished middle school, but I know I still have some more growing up to do. I'm curious about what's going to happen to me in high school. I know I'll have more freedom, but who knows what else is out there for me? I guess I'll eventually find out!"

ROB, 14

Although some adults might tell you that daydreaming is a waste of time, it's definitely not! (Unless that's *all* you do in every class at school.) Daydreams help you to:

- use your imagination
- build self-confidence
- realize that you can be a pilot, doctor, teacher, or an architect (anything you want!)
- picture yourself going anywhere or trying anything
- think about life as a spouse or parent
- prepare for your future

You may already know that dreaming only gets you so far. You also have to take action to make things happen in your life. Go for your goals, explore potential careers or educational opportunities, seek out role models and mentors, and keep believing in yourself.

Becoming proficient on the computer is also a must for the future, whether or not you plan to go to college. Being able to use a word-processing program is important, and so is the ability to find your way around the Internet to do research. It's hard to think of a job today that doesn't rely on computers in some way. Here are some examples of how computers serve as crucial tools in many fields:

- **Lawyers** use them to prepare briefs and other legal documents, or locate previous cases related to a current one.
- **Teachers** prepare lesson plans on the computer and may do Internet research to find the latest information on a topic.
- **Designers** rely on computer programs to find type fonts, add interesting graphics, and format materials such as books, magazine ads, and brochures.
- **Businesses** use computers to keep track of inventory, orders, and cash flow.
- **Authors** write original drafts on the computer, and then rewrite their drafts and edit material on screen.
- **Police** officers use computers to access information related to past records of criminals or suspects.

If you want to sharpen your computer skills, explore your school's media center, visit your local library for computer time, or take a course available through your community. The skills you learn now will help you throughout the middle-school years and beyond.

You've read through this book, thought about what other kids have said about their lives, done some of the exercises, examined your life, glanced ahead to your future, and perhaps compared notes with others who have already made their way through the middle-school years. You now have some new tools—skills, strategies, and survival tips—that you can rely on today, throughout the teen years, and even beyond.

What are the challenges and opportunities that lie ahead for you? You may be very sure that certain things will happen in your life (and some of them will), but you'll probably be surprised at how often you change your mind or your direction over the years. You'll find that situations—good and bad—will crop up unexpectedly and may cause you to adjust where you're going. Just keep using your survival tips—they're your guides to growing up successfully and moving forward in life!

"Last year, when I was in fifth grade, I was the oldest and everyone in my school seemed so little. Now I'm in middle school, and everyone seems so big. I thought that when I got to middle school I'd automatically be treated like an adult and know what to do. But it doesn't happen that way. Sometimes you get treated like you're all grown-up, but other times you're treated the same way you've always been treated. And you don't automatically have all the answers just because you're a little older. I guess there are a lot of things I still have to learn."

LIZ, 11

INDEX

· ·

ABOUT THE AUTHORS

Dr. Harriet S. Mosatche is an award-winning author of several books, including three she coauthored with her teenage daughter. As president of The Mosatche Group (mosatchegroup.com), she provides program development and evaluation support to community and national organizations that serve young people and their families. She has a doctorate in Developmental Psychology and often appears on television, radio, and the Internet, and in books, magazines, and newspapers providing expert advice. She also offers interactive workshops for tweens, teens, parents, and teachers around the United States. As online advice columnist "Dr. M" for gogirlsonly.org and studio2b.org, she receives thousands of letters monthly from girls around the world ages 6–18.

Previously a tenured college professor, psychology department chair, and Girl Scouts of the USA vice-president, Dr. Mosatche codirected research projects funded by the National Institutes of Health and the National Science Foundation. She presented her research results at conferences and in national and international journals and magazines.

Dr. Mosatche has received numerous honors and awards, including a New Rochelle Chamber of Commerce Woman of Excellence Award. Her biographical profile appears in the Marquis *Who's Who in America, Who's Who of American Women*, and *Who's Who in the East* directories, and in many other reference books. She serves on the American Bar Association Advisory Commission on Public Education and Commission for Youth at Risk.

Karen Unger is a writer and editor primarily of books for young people. In addition to *Too Old for This, Too Young for That!*, she is also the coauthor of *Where Should I Sit at Lunch? The Ultimate 24/7 Guide to Surviving the High School Years*. She has directed projects and developed many resources on matters of importance to girls and women as the manager of Program Development at Girl Scouts of the USA. Karen has also worked as a senior editor for a children's book publisher. Currently, she works as a writer at a private school and writes a column on parenting issues for a chain of weekly newspapers.

Karen once served as a Peace Corps volunteer in Liberia, West Africa, which lead to teaching English as a Second Language as a college instructor, as well as serving as the director of a college-level intensive English language program. After receiving her M.A. in English with a concentration in Creative Writing from Queens College of the City University of New York, she has had short stories based on her Liberian experiences published in magazines. When she isn't busy writing, Karen is enjoying her time with her husband and young son.

Other Great Books from Free Spirit

Stress Can Really Get on Your NERVES!

by Trevor Romain and Elizabeth Verdick
More kids than ever feel worried, stressed out, and anxious every day. Reassuring words, silly jokes, and light-hearted cartoons let them know they're not the only worry-warts on the planet—and they can learn to manage their stress. For ages 8–13.
104 pp.; softcover; illust.; 5⅛" x 7"

True or False? Tests Stink!

by Trevor Romain and Elizabeth Verdick
This book offers proven strategies and practical advice, plus plenty of humor and goofy cartoons. Kids discover tips and information that will help them survive and thrive in all kinds of test situations. For ages 8–13.
88 pp.; softcover; illust.; 5⅛" x 7"

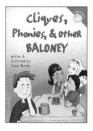

Cliques, Phonies, & Other Baloney

by Trevor Romain
Written for every kid who has ever felt excluded or trapped by a clique, this book blends humor with practical advice as it tackles a serious subject. For ages 8–13.
136 pp.; softcover; illust.; 5⅛" x 7"

How to Do Homework Without Throwing Up

written and illustrated by Trevor Romain
This book features hilarious cartoons and witty insights that teach important truths about homework and positive, practical strategies for getting it done. For ages 8–13.
72 pp.; softcover; illust.; 5⅛" x 7"

Bullies Are a Pain in the Brain

written and illustrated by Trevor Romain
Bullies are a pain in the brain—and every child needs to know what to do when confronted by one. This book combines humor with serious, practical suggestions for coping with bullies. For ages 8–13.
112 pp.; softcover; illust.; 5⅛" x 7"

Dude, That's Rude!
(Get Some Manners)
by Pamela Espeland and Elizabeth Verdick
Full-color cartoons and kid-friendly text teach the basics of polite behavior in all kinds of situations—at home, at school, and more. Kids learn Power Words to use and P.U. Words to avoid, why their family deserves their best manners, and the essentials of politeness online. Manners are major social skills, and this book gives kids a great start. For ages 8–13.
128 pp.; softcover; color illust.; 5⅛" x 7"

See You Later, Procrastinator!
(Get It Done)
by Pamela Espeland and Elizabeth Verdick
Everyone procrastinates, but it's never too late (or too soon) for kids to learn how to get stuff done, get organized, get control of their schedules, and just get started. For ages 8–13.
128 pp.; softcover; color illust.; 5⅛" x 7"

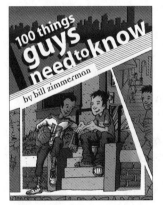

No B.O.!
The Head-to-Toe Book of Hygiene for Preteens
by Marguerite Crump, M.A., M.Ed.
This frank, reassuring, humorous book covers the physical changes of puberty and offers tips on good hygiene from head to toe. Fascinating facts, friendly suggestions, and funny illustrations combine in a lighthearted approach with strong kid appeal. For ages 9–13.
128 pp.; softcover; 2-color; illust.; 7" x 9"

100 Things Guys Need to Know
by Bill Zimmerman
Advice for guys on all kids of issues, from family life to fitting in, emotions, bullies, school, peer pressure, failure, anger, and more. Graphic-novel-style illustrations engage even reluctant readers. Quotes from boys, survey results, facts, and stories keep them interested. Journaling prompts personalize the experience. Conversation starters for adults are available as a *free download* at our Web site. For boys ages 9–13.
128 pp.; softcover; 2-color; illust.; 8" x 10½"